# 100
## CREATIVE TECHNIQUES
### FOR
## TEACHING BIBLE STORIES

PHYLLIS VOS WEZEMAN

# Dedication

*To the colleagues who served on the Board of Directors of Phoenix
Power and Light Company, Inc. (Phoenix Performing Arts Ministries)
during my two terms (1993/1994 and 1994/1995) as President:*

| | | |
|---|---|---|
| *Albert Alter* | *Diane Finley* | *Bruce Nolin* |
| *Laura Bender* | *Emma Lee Hartle* | *Jaime Rickert* |
| *Rosalie Branigan* | *Pat Hutchinson* | *Ruth Turk* |
| *Carolyn Costley* | *Karen Kraft* | *Kay Turner* |
| *Don DeNoon* | *Dave Mura* | |

*... with gratitude for your commitment to telling the story in so many ways!!!*

*P.V.W.*

ISBN 978-1-949628-02-9
Printed in the United States of America.
10 9 8 7 6 5 4 3 2 1   22 21 20 19 18

The Scripture passages contained herein are from the *New Revised Standard Version of the Bible*, copyright © 1989, by the Division of Christian Education of the National Council of Churches in the U.S.A. All rights reserved.

# Contents

# Overview

"I love to tell the story!" The words of an old hymn say it well. Throughout the centuries the church has told of God's love through the medium of the story. Storytelling has been, and continues to be, an integral part of the ministries of worship, education, nurture, and outreach of every parish.

Pause for a few minutes to think about storytelling. Take a piece of paper and a pen or a pencil. Divide the paper into five columns. Write one of the following lines across the top of each section:

- **WHY** tell stories?
- **WHERE/WHEN** are stories told?
- **WHAT** types of stories are used?
- **WHO** is the audience?
- **WHAT** are some methods of telling stories?

Next, take one minute per column and brainstorm a list of answers to each question.

For example, responses to **WHY** might include:

- Jesus was a storyteller;
- people listen to stories;

- stories are fun.

Ideas for **WHERE** could be:

- Sunday School;
- Vacation Bible School;
- Weekday classes.

**TYPES** include:

- Bible stories;
- folk tales;
- oral traditions.

Of course, the **WHO** is:

- everyone;
- people of all ages;
- US!

*100 Creative Techniques for Teaching Bible Stories* is a book that offers more than one hundred answers to the question "WHAT are some TECHNIQUES of telling stories?" Each of the ten chapters highlights a particular method of storytelling including Art, Banners/Textiles, Creative Writing, Dance/Gesture/Movement, Drama, Games, Music, Photography, Puppetry, and Storytelling. Each method contains ten ideas for "telling the story" through this approach. Even though specific examples might be suggested, in general, each of the methods may be adapted to any story.

Provided in an easy to use format, each suggestion is organized into two parts—Materials and Method. "Materials" lists the required supplies and offers suggestions for advance preparation, where needed. "Method" contains directions for accomplishing the task.

Perhaps you have some questions about using this resource. Let's consider a few ways that it will be helpful to the volunteer teacher leading a religion lesson in a parish setting.

Maybe you are one of those religious education volunteers who works from a prescribed curriculum or a purchased textbook to teach a class. The instructions are clear about what story to tell and the basic information that you need to convey, but you are looking for some way to make the lesson more meaningful, as well as more memorable. For example, at Christmas the lesson is easily determined, but you want to do something other than create the fifth annual Christmas crèche mobile.

Your assignment, for example, is to teach the annunciation—Gabriel's announcement to Mary that she is to conceive and bear a son. Knowing the group you work with, you want to enhance the basic lesson you are given which focuses mostly on the comprehension of the angelic message. You want to involve the learners in the story so that they will appreciate the thrill and challenge of God's plan for Mary's life—and for their lives as well. That's the point at which this book becomes an extremely helpful resource.

Thinking about the story of the annunciation, then, you would review the techniques presented in this book and look at the specific options that would be most helpful for you to use. For example, you might want to focus on using body language to help participants enter into the feelings that Mary experienced in the presence of God's messenger. Or, maybe creative writing would be an appropriate way for reflecting upon God's plan for each life.

The techniques described can also be used to open, enrich, expand, or conclude any lesson when a teacher needs five or ten minutes of ideas to adapt the class schedule. You will use this book as an extension for enhancing, as well as for planning lessons.

Let's consider another situation. You may be a religious education teacher who is free to select the story you want to tell based on the season of the church year or the focus of a particular program. However, just knowing the focus for a lesson is not enough. Effective teachers know that a lesson has key elements that guide student learning from the introduction of an objective to a meaningful outcome. They accept responsibility for planning each lesson, much like an accomplished cook plans a balanced menu from appetizer to dessert.

You decide, for example, that you want to focus on the stories of meals Jesus shared as preparation for a first communion class. The first one you choose is the "Feeding of the Five Thousand." Knowing your group, you decide that you want to use an interactive approach to convey the importance of offering our gifts to God, like the little boy offered the five loaves and the two fish to feed the crowd. This book can help you plan each key element of a successful lesson.

You want to find something catchy to introduce the lesson and the objective. So you sift through the ten chapters contained in the book—filled with over one hundred suggestions—and decide to use music as an opener. An idea in the chapter on "Telling the Story through Music" inspires you to write simple words to a familiar tune to introduce the message and sequence of the miracle God gave by the Sea of Galilee. Next you select drama and photography as the methods to recreate the meaning, deciding to improvise and video an "eyewitness account" of the miracle. To review the critical concept, you choose the creative writing approach of a "diamond poem," using the words "hungry" and "fed" as the opposites in the suggested pattern. As closure, you will ask your students to draw a picture of a gift that they can give to God as they prepare to receive their first communion.

The beauty of this book is that no matter your teaching situation and no matter the lesson assigned, you can use and re-use the contents to find a fresh approach to telling the story and, ultimately, to help your learners make it their story. Jesus used storytelling as his primary teaching tool. He improvised the lesson based on his listeners and their needs. While none of us can expect to teach like the Master, we can adopt a more flexible approach that allows creativity and innovation to guide our lesson preparation and presentation.

While the activities in *100 Creative Techniques* are mainly intended for learners in a classroom, they may be easily adapted for use by children, youth, and adults in small and large group settings. They are ideal for religious education classes, parochial school programs, vacation Bible school courses, confirmation sessions, intergenerational events, youth groups, retreat settings, family devotions, home schooling, and more.

As you use this resource, may you find many ways to share biblical stories, contemporary stories, historical stories, and your own personal stories in order to claim God's story as your own.

# Telling the Story through Art

It's a good thing there are lots of stories to tell: there are so many art techniques to use to tell them!  Any art method, such as papier mâché or plaster molding, pottery or printmaking, can be used to recite, review, or reinforce a story.  Art projects offer an excellent way to educate for content, but more importantly, they provide an opportunity to explore and express thoughts and feelings through participation in the process.

The ten ideas presented in this chapter are only a starting point.  Numerous other art methods should be incorporated into lesson preparation and presentation.  For example, a rebus story activity might suggest drawing illustrations to represent words in the narrative, a creative writing exercise could recommend having the learners make a collage of their reactions and responses, and a puppetry project may direct the group to paint interesting characters, props, and scenery.  Regardless of the method used, try telling the story through art!

# Acquire the Art

## Materials

- ▸ Art history books
- ▸ Bible(s)
- ▸ Illustrations
- ▸ Pictures

## Method

Save and use art from a variety of sources: book jackets, bulletin covers, curriculum illustrations, and teaching pictures. Mount the pictures and highlight them as examples while telling a story, hang them on bulletin boards to introduce a theme, or use them as flash cards to help the students review a lesson. Include art from a variety of historical periods, which may be found on posters and prints as well as in reference materials and textbooks. Help the learners observe some of the ways in which artists through the ages have portrayed the scenes from various stories.

# Color with Chalk

## Materials

- ▸ Bible(s)
- ▸ Chalk
- ▸ Chalkboard or window(s)
- ▸ Containers for water
- ▸ Paper
- ▸ Pencils or pens
- ▸ Water

## Method

Do a chalk talk on a traditional surface such as a chalkboard or on a unique background like a window. If windows are selected, use many panes to depict various parts of a Scripture passage. Be sure to obtain permission to use the glass and clean it when finished with the project. It may be helpful to sketch the design on paper before beginning the work on the windows. Use wet chalk to draw the pictures on the glass. Images can range from full scenes to stick figures. Pictures may be drawn at an appropriate point in the telling of the story, as an introduction to the theme, or as a review of a lesson or unit.

# Design a Dial

*Materials*

- ► Bible(s)
- ► Markers
- ► Metal paper fasteners
- ► Paper plates
- ► Pencils
- ► Scissors

## Method

Turn two paper plates into a story dial. Make the top section by cutting the rim off of one of the plates. Divide this circle into equal sections, which may be small or large, depending on the number of scenes required for the story. Illustrate each section by drawing or gluing pictures on the segments. Center the circle with the pictures on top of the other plate. Attach the two plates by inserting a metal paper fastener in the middle of the pieces. Draw an arrow, point down, at the top of the outer edge. As the story is told, turn the dial to the appropriate picture. Larger or smaller story dials, for group and individual projects, may be made from cardboard, poster board, or various types of paper. Try a mini-dial as a wristband.

# Do a Diorama

*Materials*

- ► Bible(s)
- ► Construction paper
- ► Glue
- ► Paint (optional)
- ► Paint brushes (optional)
- ► Shoe boxes
- ► Scissors

## Method

Recreate the scenes of a story by constructing individual or group dioramas, a scenic display of figures against a background. Each participant may make his or her own shoe box scene or the whole class may build one in a large cardboard carton.

Review the story with the learners and help each person decide which part of it to depict.

To make a diorama, set the box on its side so that the bottom of the box becomes the back of the scene. Cover the outside of the carton with paint or paper. Create a background on the inside of the box by cutting, drawing, or painting a scene on the cardboard. Illustrate the story with clay sculptures, clothespin people, or paper cutouts.

# Flip the Facts

## Materials

- Bible(s)
- Hole punch
- Markers
- Newsprint
- Overhead projector (optional)
- Pencils
- Poster board
- Ribbon
- Sticky notes (optional)

## Method

Illustrate the main parts of a story on full sheets of poster board or newsprint and make a flip chart out of them. If diagrams or patterns are used, project the designs on a wall with an overhead machine. Trace the shapes onto the paper. Create a 3-D effect on the pages by adding textured fabric, paper, and other materials. Punch holes in the top of each picture and tie the sheets together with ribbon, string, or yarn. Flip the pages to tell the story.

Invite the participants to review the message by making mini-flip charts on sticky notes.

# Form Some Flannelgraph

## Materials

- Bible(s)
- Cardboard or plywood
- Crayons
- Felt, flannel, or indoor/outdoor carpeting
- Interfacing fabric
- Patterns for figures
- Pencils
- Scissors
- Stapler and staples (heavy-duty)

## Method

Construct the background for the story by covering a piece of cardboard or plywood with felt, flannel, or indoor-outdoor carpeting. Staple the material in place.

Prepare figure patterns by cutting pictures from used church school papers or religious coloring books. Trace the people onto interfacing fabric, a stiff material used in sewing. Use crayons to color and highlight the pieces. Cut them out. Children's drawings or other paper figures may be used instead. Back them with sandpaper or felt to make them adhere to the background material. (Ready-made commercial sets of flannelboard figures and scenery in large sizes and bright colors, may be purchased in craft stores or online.)

# Model a Mobile

## Materials

► Bible(s)
► Construction paper or poster board
► Hangers
► Hole punches
► Markers
► Pencils or pens
► Ribbon, string, or yarn
► Scissors

## Method

Make a mobile and use the pieces to tell a story or to help learners make their own mobiles to review a story. Cut shapes from construction paper or poster board. The shapes may represent the message or the symbolism of the story. Write, draw, or cut and paste information on the pieces such as: title, Scripture verse, symbols representing parts of the passage, and scenes from the story. Punch a hole at the top of each shape and string a length of ribbon, string, or yarn through it. Tie the pieces to a hanger and display the mobile.

# Piece a Puzzle

## Materials

► Bible(s)
► Envelopes
► Markers
► Pencils or pens
► Poster board
► Scissors

## Method

Cut a large shape or symbol associated with a significant part of a story. For the account of Noah, the obvious one is an ark. A sheep may illustrate David's early life, and a manger could represent the Christmas Scriptures. Cut the large shape into jigsaw puzzle pieces. Place the pieces for each puzzle in a separate envelope.

Put the puzzle pieces together to teach the lesson. Connect the symbol and the story. Name the object being made and the Scripture being shared.

# Sequence the Story

## Materials

- Bible(s)
- Construction paper
- Glue
- Fabric scraps
- Magazines
- Markers
- Paper, individual sheets or rolls
- Tacks or tape
- Scissors

## Method

Depict the details of a Bible story by making a mural. Individual sheets as well as rolls of butcher, shelf, or tablecloth paper work well for the background. Tack or tape the paper to a bulletin board or a wall.

Illustrate the scenes in sequence with figures torn from paper, objects cut from fabric, pictures taken from magazines, or items drawn with chalk, crayons, markers, or paint.

Use the mural to set the mood, sequence the events, or to see if the participants have comprehended the story's message.

# View a Video Box

## Materials

- Bible(s)
- Carton(s)
- Craft knife
- Dowel rods
- Paper, individual sheets or roll
- Tape

## Method

A video box is a technique that combines a series of drawings, which tell a story, with a method for showing them that is similar to a television screen. Begin constructing a video box by tucking in or cutting off the flaps of a carton. Using a mat knife cut a large square out of the center of the bottom of the box, leaving a two to three inch border around the entire area. Turn the box on its side, so that the bottom now becomes the front, or viewing area. Make a set of parallel holes on the top and bottom of the box on both sides of the window. Place a dowel rod through each set of holes. Secure them in place with tape or a cardboard or wooden stop.

Select a story and illustrate each part of it on individual papers or a roll of adding machine tape, shelf liner, tablecloth, or wrapping paper. Attach the beginning of the mural to one dowel and the end to the other. Wind the mural through the box to tell the story.

# Telling the Story through Banners/Textiles

Banners and textile projects, with and without words, may be used to proclaim messages pertaining to biblical themes. In essence, banners are stories illustrated on material.

Banners have interesting biblical and historical significance. Banners were carried by the Egyptians in 5,000 B.C. Streamers were attached to long poles and carried into battle to appeal to the gods for assistance. Romans attached banners to spears. The words "banner" and "standard" in the Old Testament seem to refer to modern day flags. Often made from wood, leather, or metal, they were used as a means of identification of a person, family, or group. During the Middle Ages, tapestries of wool, linen, and silk were an important part of the church. Not only were they beautiful works of art, they also served as insulation in cold buildings and as teaching tools for the people, most of whom could not read or write. An image of the cross was first carried on Constantine's banner in the fourth century. It served as a morale booster for the early Christians.

Banners may be constructed from almost any fabric, even paper. The type of material is often determined by whether the piece will be used inside or outside. Color, a critical factor in the impact a banner will make, should be a consideration in selecting the material. The design can be sewn on by hand or machine, or glued into place. The space in which a banner will hang determines the size of the project. In a small space, use a banner that will not look crowded. In a large area, make sure it is big enough to be seen. Hang the banner on a dowel or curtain rod, broom handle or wire, or an object that accents the theme.

▶

Display banners in worship spaces, classrooms, social halls, and entrances, and in schoolrooms, gyms, and hallways. In the community, hang banners in empty storefront windows, on banner poles on the street, or carry them in community parades and neighborhood walks. At home, display banners inside and outside of the house.

Banners can be powerful means of communicating the message of God's love. Ten banner and textile suggestions for telling the story through this media are offered in this chapter. Projects range from items that can be made by individuals and pieces that could be put together by groups. Tell the story through banners!

# Begin with a Branch

## Materials

- ▶ Bible(s)
- ▶ Branches
- ▶ Items related to story

## Method

Vary the material used in making a banner to match its theme. For example, when depicting Galatians 5, the Fruit of the Spirit, a Jesse Tree showing the lineage of Jesus, or the Genesis 1 Creation story, use a large branch or even a real or silk tree. Branches can become the base of a group project, and smaller limbs can be used for individual designs. Cut shapes from interesting materials, or use objects as symbols, and hang them on the branches. Celebrate the joy of Jesus' resurrection by decorating the limbs with bright streamers, tissue paper flowers, and other signs of new life.

Carry the branch banners in a procession, or plant them in appropriate containers and place them throughout the classroom, worship space, building, and grounds.

# Bring the Bags

## Materials

- ▶ Bags, resealable plastic
- ▶ Bible(s)
- ▶ Construction paper
- ▶ Dowel rods
- ▶ Glue
- ▶ Items related to the story
- ▶ Ribbon, string, or yarn
- ▶ Tape

## Method

Visualize the scenes or the sequence of a story by placing objects or pictures related to it in clear plastic bags. Join the bags together to form a long vertical or horizontal strip.

Begin by finding items or photos, or by drawing or constructing illustrations that represent the parts of the passage. For example, to highlight the parable of the sower and the seed use things such as rocks, thorns, and soil. Place one item in each baggie. Objects may be glued to construction paper cut to fit the inside of each bag. Seal the tops.

Tape the bags to each other, front and back, to create a long banner. Letters can be glued inside or outside the bags. Fold the top of the first bag over a dowel rod and tape it in place. Attach yarn, string, or ribbon to the ends of the dowel to hang the banner.

Although the see-through effect will not be achieved, paper and plastic bags, in various sizes, shapes, and patterns, may also be used as banner backgrounds.

# Conceive with Computer

## Materials

- ▶ Bible(s)
- ▶ Computer
- ▶ Markers
- ▶ Printer
- ▶ Software for banners

## Method

Thanks to technology there are numerous techniques for making banners. All that's needed is a computer, a software package, and a printer. Long strip messages, as well as individual sheets fastened together, may display letter or symbol designs. Enhance and emphasize words and pictures by coloring them with pencils or markers. To make banners more permanent, cover them with laminating film.

Choose a story and illustrate its theme with a computer banner. To spark interest and attention, hang the piece in the classroom before the participants arrive and use it to introduce the lesson. Or, design an activity in which everyone can participate by making individual banners or group projects. Display the results for others to enjoy.

# Find Some Fabric

## Materials

- ▶ Bible(s)
- ▶ Fabric
- ▶ Glue
- ▶ Scissors
- ▶ Sewing machine (optional)
- ▶ Yardstick

## Advance Preparation

- ▶ Prepare banner background.

## Method

Make fabric banners to set the mood for a meeting, proclaim a story visually, affirm a biblical truth, or identify a special event. Although burlap and felt are commonly used as banner backgrounds, there are many other types of materials from which to choose. Try upholstery or drapery fabrics, corduroy, monks cloth, castle cloth, or velveteen. Lining options may be firm cottons or cotton blends, poplin, Indian head, or kettle cloth.

To prepare a fabric background, press the material and straighten it as needed. Measure the desired size and cut on the straight of the grain. If the banner is to be lined, add two inches to the width and length of its finished size. If the banner is to have a casing at the top, add four inches to the height. Provide extra length at the bottom for fringe.

Create original designs to tell a story or use an overhead projector or copier to enlarge existing patterns. Cut letters and shapes from various materials. Lay out the entire banner before gluing or sewing anything in place. Re-arrange as needed and secure the pieces to the background.

# Produce Some Paper

## Materials

- ► Bible(s)
- ► Dowels
- ► Glue
- ► Magazines
- ► Markers
- ► Paper, various sizes and types
- ► Pencils and pens
- ► Scissors
- ► String

## Method

Paper (poster board, newsprint, computer, butcher, and more) can be used to produce banners that portray stories. Find paper in various sizes, colors, and textures for banner backgrounds. Attach the top of the paper to a stick or string for easy hanging or tape the piece(s) directly to a wall.

Symbols, words, pictures, and designs may be added to the background by using various techniques. Glue shapes of torn paper or cut out pictures to illustrate a story. Pick one theme and use markers, crayons, or colored pencils to depict a story. Create three-dimensional designs by adding pieces with paper techniques such as origami, fabric, and other materials. Add texture by placing the paper on a surface, such as a leaf, and rubbing over it evenly with a crayon.

Match the banner background and the message. For example, tell the good news of the resurrection by pasting words and symbols on a piece of newspaper. Make some banners large for group projects or use individual creations as doorknob hangers.

# Put Together Pieces

## Materials

- ► Bible(s)
- ► Construction paper or fabric
- ► Fabric paints or permanent markers
- ► Glue or tape
- ► Scissors
- ► Sewing equipment (optional)

## Method

Begin with pieces of fabric that can be combined into a large banner, table covering, or wall hanging. Distribute a portion to each person or small group. Instruct the participants to use a pencil to lightly draw a scene, shape, or symbol from a story on the fabric. Paint it with fabric paint or permanent markers. Glue, sew, or tape the sections together.

Display the completed banner in a prominent place to remind the participants, and the congregation, of the message of the story.

# Remember with Ribbon

## Materials

- ► Bible(s)
- ► Dowel rods
- ► Permanent markers
- ► Ribbon
- ► Scissors
- ► Tacks or tape

## Method

As a way of reviewing a story, make a ribbon banner. Try this idea as an individual or group project. The same story may be illustrated by each student on separate pieces of ribbon that can be taken home or the lengths could be attached to one rod that remains in the classroom. Another option is to depict a different Scripture passage on each ribbon.

To begin, cut the ribbon to the desired length and distribute the pieces to the participants. Choose a keyword or memory verse from the lesson and use permanent marker to write it on the strip. Or, cut one shape or many symbols representing various parts of the story from paper, felt, or vinyl and attach them to the ribbon. For example, for the life of Noah, use the key word "faith" or symbols such as a hammer, ark, animals, water, altar, and rainbow.

As a class project, make one ribbon each week to reinforce the theme. Attach them to a rod with tape or tacks. The ribbons may flow freely or they can be anchored to a rod across the bottom. Display the ribbon banner in a prominent place.

# Start with a Shade

## Materials

- ► Bible(s)
- ► Fabric scraps
- ► Glue
- ► Paint
- ► Paint brushes
- ► Permanent markers
- ► Scissors
- ► Window shade(s)

## Method

Available in various widths and lengths, as well as colors and patterns, window shades make great banner backgrounds. They're the right size, come with finished edges, and already have the poles in place. Pull one down or roll one out and create a design. Use paints, permanent markers, or pieces of fabric to express the chosen theme.

Surprise the students by preparing scenes from a story on several shades and pulling them down at the appropriate point during the storytelling. As an additional or alternative activity, use shades as banner backgrounds and have individuals or groups design projects to tell the story.

# Stitch a Symbol

## Materials

► Bible(s)
► Chalk
► Embroidery needles
► Fabric
► Glue
► Yarn

## Advance Preparation

► Prepare banner background.

## Method

Stitch a scene or a symbol from a story on a pre-made banner background. With chalk, make a line drawing on the material. Using heavy yarn and an embroidery needle, chain stitch along the chalk line.

As an alternative, "stitch" without using a needle and thread with a similar method. On a prepared background, write a word or draw an object with chalk. Squeeze a line of white glue along the chalk line and attach the yarn to the glue. Display the finished piece.

# Wax a Windsock

## Materials

► Bible(s)
► Brown paper
► Brushes
► Cans
► Dye
► Electric skillet or warming tray
► Fabric paints
► Glue
► Hole punch
► Iron
► Melted bees wax
► Muslin
► Paraffin
► Pencils
► Permanent markers
► Poster board
► Scissors
► Stapler & staples
► String
► Water

## Method

Express the essence of a story with colors or symbols by using Batik, an Indonesian fabric technique. Batik is a method of layering wax and dye on cloth to create works of art. Create a batik windsock or kite to use as a banner.

Sketch a design on a piece of muslin. Use fabric paints or permanent markers to color the entire drawing. Heat a mixture of one-half paraffin and one-half melted beeswax and brush it over the entire surface of the cloth. After it has hardened, wrinkle the piece until the wax cracks. Reopen the cloth. Slide the waxed cloth into a solution of cold water dye, remove it, and allow the piece to air dry. Place the dry cloth between sheets of brown paper and iron it with a warm iron until the wax in the cloth is absorbed into the paper. Remove the paper.

Staple or glue poster board strips to the top and bottom of the windsock to stabilize the cloth. Overlap the side seams and glue them together. Add streamers to the bottom as decorations and string to the top as a hanger.

# Telling the Story
## through
## Creative Writing

Tell the Bible story through poetry! Besides the rhyme and rhythm, the variety of styles of poetry make this a particularly attractive method to use with children, youth, and adults. Participants appreciate hearing the compositions of others.

Poetry can be used as a storytelling method for numerous lessons and in a number of learning situations. Ten ideas and activities to help participants explore biblical themes and concepts through poetry are provided. There are many other poetry formats and formulas to try, too. Experiment, express, and educate by telling the story through poetry.

# Celebrate God's Creation: Haiku

## Materials

- Bible(s)
- Crayons, colored pencils, or markers
- Formula for Haiku poetry
- Paper
- Pencils or pens

## Method

A Haiku is an unrhymed Japanese poem of three lines. It is usually light and delicate in feeling and is concerned with something lovely in nature, especially the seasons of the year.

The formula for Haiku is:

- Line One: *Five syllables*
- Line Two: *Seven syllables*
- Line Three: *Five syllables*

Write Haiku poems that express praise to God for various seasons of the year. An example involving summer is:

**Warm temperatures**
**Bright sun; Beautiful flowers**
**Summertime is here.**

If desired, use colored pencils, crayons, or markers to draw illustrations that will enhance the theme.

# Clarify a Concept: ABC

## Materials

- Bible(s)
- Formula for ABC poetry
- Paper
- Pencils or pens

## Method

ABC poetry is written in a short form and expresses strong emotion. The initial letters of the beginning words in the first four lines are written alphabetically, for example C, D, E, F or M, N, O, P. The first line does not have to begin with A.

In these two examples, the formula for ABC poetry is:

- Line One—Line Four: *Clauses beginning with four consecutive letters*
- Line Five: *A sentence beginning with any letter.*

Help children understand a biblical concept, such as faith, by writing ABC poetry. For example:

**Faith**
**God's guidance**
**Hope for the future**
**Incredible love**
**Belief in the Savior.**

# Learn the Lesson: Quatrain

## Materials

- Bible(s)
- Formula for Quatrain poetry
- Glue
- Magazines
- Paper
- Pencils or pens
- Scissors

## Method

Quatrains are four line poems that may follow any one of four different rhyme patterns:

### AABB

*Lines One (A) and Two (A) end with words that rhyme.*

*Lines Three (B) and Four (B) end with words that rhyme.*

### ABAB

*Lines One (A) and Three (A) end with words that rhyme.*

*Lines Two (B) and Four (B) end with words that rhyme.*

### ABBA

*Lines One (A) and Four (A) end with words that rhyme.*

*Lines Two (B) and Three (B) end with words that rhyme.*

### ABCB

*Line One (A) does not rhyme with the other three lines.*

*Lines Two (B) and Four (B) end with words that rhyme.*

*Line Three (C) does not rhyme with the other three.*

When Quatrains are combined to make a long poem, each group of four lines is called a stanza. Use Quatrains to teach the stories of great persons of faith: past, present, and future. It might be helpful to cut pictures from magazines and to write verses about these people. Using the life of Mother Theresa as an example, a Quatrain with an ABCB rhyming pattern might read:

Mother Theresa helped the poor,
she offered loving care.
She shared God's love in many ways
with people everywhere.

# Make Verses Meaningful: Lantern

## Materials

► Bible(s)
► Formula for Lantern poetry
► Paper
► Pencils or Pens

## Method

A Lantern poem is a light and airy Oriental style of creative writing that is printed in the shape of a Japanese lantern. The structure for a Lantern poem is:

► Line One: *One syllable*
► Line Two: *Two syllables*
► Line Three: *Three syllables*
► Line Four: *Four syllables*
► Line Five: *One syllable*

Use Lantern poetry as a way to explore and express the meaning of a memory verse. For example, adapting the words of the familiar New Testament text John 3:16, "For God so loved the world that he gave his only Son, so that everyone who believes in him may not perish but may have eternal life," the Lantern poem might read:

Love

Jesus

Salvation

For all people

Gift.

# Paraphrase a Psalm: Cinquain

## Materials

► Bible(s)
► Formula for Cinquain poetry
► Paper
► Pencils or pens

## Method

Cinquain is a simple, five line verse form. Its structure follows specific rules:

► Line One: *One word of two syllables (may be the title)*
► Line Two: *Four syllables (describes the subject or title)*
► Line Three: *Six syllables (shows action)*
► Line Four: *Eight syllables (expresses a feeling or observation about the subject)*
► Line Five: *Two syllables (describes or renames the subject)*

After reading a Psalm, paraphrase it by writing Cinquain poems. The members of the group may select the same or different Psalms. An example using Psalm 8 is:

**Heavens**

**Filled with wonder**

**Formed with sun, moon, and stars**

**Displaying the greatness of God**

**Mighty.**

# Pen a Prayer: Couplet

## Materials

► Bible(s)
► Formula for Couplet poetry
► Hymnal
► Paper
► Pencils or pens

## Method

Couplets follow a simple pattern and consist of two rhyming lines. Lines can be any length, and the rhythm and rhyme should match the thought or mood of the poem. Use this easy style to write prayers, such as:

**My good friend Tim is very sick**
**Please help him to get better quick.**

Many stanzas of hymns are in couplet form. Illustrate this by showing examples and offering some of these lines as prayers, too. Using two lines from the favorite carol, "Away In a Manger," the prayer would be:

**"Be with me Lord Jesus,**
**I ask thee to stay,**
**Close by me forever,**
**and love me I pray."**

# Select a Season: Dada

## Materials

► Bible(s)
► Bowl
► Formula for Dada poetry
► Glue
► Magazines
► Newspaper
► Paper
► Pencils or pens
► Scissors

## Method

Dada poetry was originally written by artists and poets in Paris, France who clipped words from newspapers, scrambled them, and then arranged them in lines to form verses. Express the essence of a season of the Church Year, such as Easter, through this form of creative writing. Write down or cut out ten verbs, such as alive or arose; eight nouns, for example, Jesus, angel, and disciples; and some articles like a, an, and the. Jumble them up in a bowl and draw them out one at a time. Arrange the words on a piece of paper until they form an Easter message. Glue them in place.

# Share an Old Testament Story: Alliteration

## Materials

- Bible(s)
- Formula for Alliteration poetry
- Paper
- Pencils or pens

## Method

Alliteration is the repetition of a sound in two or more neighboring words. In this type of poetry, there is the same beginning letter for every word in the row. Alliteration poems may be one or more lines, rhymed or unrhymed. Respond to an Old Testament story, like David and Goliath, by writing Alliterative poetry, such as:

**David's daring decision**
**Face ferocious foe**
**God's gracious guidance**
**Turned trust to triumph.**

# Suggest a Solution: Diamond

## Materials

- Bible(s)
- Formula for Diamond poetry
- Paper
- Pencils or pens

## Method

Share a current event story, which presents a problem such as care of the environment, and come up with creative solutions through a poetry project. Use a five-line diamond shaped poem for this process. The formula for Diamond poetry is as follows:

- Line One: *One word which is an opposite of line five*
- Line Two: *Two words which describe line one*
- Line Three: *Three words which resolve the conflict*
- Line Four: *Two words which describe line five*
- Line Five: *One word which is an opposite of line one*

For example:

**Litter**
**Garbage everywhere**
**New uses found**
**Gather.  Collect.**
**Recycle.**

# Try a Theme: Tanka

## Materials

- ▶ Bible(s)
- ▶ Formula for Tanka poetry
- ▶ Paper
- ▶ Pencils or pens

## Method

Tanka is another Oriental verse form much like Haiku except that two more lines of seven syllables each are added to give this type of poetry a total of thirty-one syllables. The format for Tanka poetry is:

- ▶ Line One: *Five syllables*
- ▶ Line Two: *Seven syllables*
- ▶ Line Three: *Five syllables*
- ▶ Line Four: *Seven syllables*
- ▶ Line Five: *Seven syllables*

Use the Tanka formula to help the participants share their own stories. Suggest that everyone write a Tanka describing him or herself. For example:

Mrs. Stevenson
Teacher; Guide; Friend; Example
Shows concern and care
Prepares exciting lessons
Listens; Laughs; Learns; Loves;
and Leads.

# Telling the Story through Dance/Gesture/Movement

"Dance has the power to renew—to enliven—to draw a people together. Dancing people are people who can feel the Spirit quicken within them, and face the future with hope." (Adelaide Ortegal, *A Dancing People*, p. 1.) Dance, therefore, is a powerful medium to use in storytelling. Symbolic expression of the human body sometimes reaches the hearts and souls of people more effectively than spoken or sung messages.

A traditional form of worship in the early Christian Church, dance can be used in conjunction with prayers, readings, and songs to raise the level of spiritual awareness about the theme of most any Scripture story. Used in education, dance, gesture, and movement can help participants explore and experience a variety of concepts and themes.

Dance, both formal steps and informal actions, is available to everyone. Inexperienced and trained dancers can share equally in creating movements and pieces that range from simple to elaborate, from concrete to abstract. Ten learning activities using dance methods are suggested in this chapter. Declare the story through dance!

# Circle the Content

## Materials

- ▶ Bible(s)
- ▶ Camera (optional)
- ▶ Envelopes
- ▶ Equipment to play music
- ▶ Index cards, 3" x 5"
- ▶ Pencils or pens
- ▶ Pictures of people using their hands to help people (optional)
- ▶ Projector (optional)
- ▶ Recording of "Healing Hands" by Elton John
- ▶ Screen (optional)

## Advance Preparation

Take or find pictures of people using their hands to help other people. (optional)

Practice projecting and coordinating the pictures and the background music. (optional)

Write one word of a Bible verse on each index card. Place the cards for each verse in a separate envelope. Some possible verses are:

- ▶ Matthew 8:3 – Healing the leper
- ▶ Mark 5:41 – Healing Jairus' daughter
- ▶ Mark 10:16 – Jesus blesses the children
- ▶ John 9:6 – Healing the man born blind
- ▶ Matthew 8:15 – Healing Peter's mother-in-law

## Method

Dozens of stories in the New Testament demonstrate ways in which Jesus included the people that most others excluded. Invite the participants to review Scripture passages that illustrate Jesus' actions and attitudes of including everyone in the circle of God's love.

Explain that the words of several Bible verses have been written on separate index cards and that they must be put in order before they can be read. Determine whether the students will work alone or in small groups for this portion of the activity. Distribute an envelope to each person or team. Tell the learners that the envelopes contain the words of a New Testament verse related to Jesus' care for people. One word of the verse is written on each card in the envelope. The challenge is to put the words together in the proper order to form the verse. Once the learners think that the words are in order, they may use a Bible to check their work. Provide time for everyone to finish this portion of the activity. Once completed, allow the students to share their passages.

Talk with the students about people today who need to be included rather than excluded. Mention individuals affected by AIDS, refugees from another country, people who are physically challenged, and so forth. Since Jesus is no longer on the earth, ask the group who can provide this important ministry. Of course, the answer is God's people today. Let the participants share their thoughts on this topic.

Play the song "Healing Hands" by Elton John and show the pictures of people using their hands to help other people. If there are no pictures, play the song and ask the group to listen to the words. Play the song again and invite the participants to illustrate this

100 CREATIVE TECHNIQUES FOR TEACHING BIBLE STORIES

theme in the form of a circle dance. Ask the students to hold hands and to form a circle, however, leave three or four people out of the ring. Turn on the music and invite those in the circle to move to an easy dance step such as:

**One step in, bend at the knee**
**One step out, bend at the knee**
**One step to the right, bend at the knee**

Direct the dancers to continue the movement, holding hands at all times. Remind them that if they drop hands it might permit the "left-out" persons to join the circle. Encourage the students to do the same dance, dropping hands for the second round and giving the left-out children an opportunity to step into the circle.

Talk about what it felt like to allow someone to come into the circle. Discuss ways that attitudes and behavior invite people in or keep them out of a variety of day-to-day activities. Remind the group that the Christian's response should always be one of inviting people into the circle of God's love.

# Demonstrate with Dance

## Materials

► Bible(s)
► Equipment to play music
► Information on organization(s)
► Paper or notebooks
► Pencils or pens
► Recordings of selected music
► Snacks
► Sponsor sheets

## Advance Preparation

Designate the organization to receive the collection.

Enlist personnel to chaperone the event, to lead the dances, and to run the equipment.

Prepare and distribute sponsor sheets.

## Method

Live a lesson, such as Matthew 25—ministering in Jesus' name to the hungry, the thirsty, the stranger, the sick, the poor, and the imprisoned by holding a dance event to demonstrate commitment to a cause. Funds raised through this type of function benefit agencies that provide services such as education, housing, meals, and medicine.

Encourage the students to prepare and present a Dance-a-Thon for a cause. Discuss the selected Scripture story, such as Matthew 25:35-36, and identify agencies that feed the hungry and shelter the stranger. Name organizations that care for the sick and minister to the imprisoned. Contact various groups to obtain information, as well as resources and speakers. Select the date, time, and place for a Dance-a-Thon. Begin on a Friday evening and run non-stop through Saturday night, or hold the activity for a morning, afternoon, evening, or an entire day. Secure chaperones and leaders as well as guest artists or celebrity dancers for the event.

Preparations for a Dance-a-Thon must begin in several ways. If part of the purpose of the event is to raise funds for a specific ministry, prepare sponsor sheets and distribute them to the participants. Challenge the group to find people who will pledge money for each minute, half-hour, or hour that they dance. Gather music from various sources. Secure the required equipment. Distribute it throughout the building, designating rooms for different age levels. Ask participants to bring a notebook and a pen or pencil to record their dance times. Suggest that they bring pillows, sleeping bags, and snacks.

At the beginning of the Dance-a-Thon, gather the group and explain the policies and procedures. Note that each person must keep track of his or her own dance time. Encourage everyone to keep dancing until the time runs out, stopping only for snacks, speakers, and stretches. If varying age groups are involved, assign people to designated rooms.

At the conclusion of the event, instruct the participants to collect pledges and to return them to a designated person by a specific date. Report on ways in which funds raised during the Dance-a-Thon were used to share the story.

# Focus on Folk

## Materials

- Bible(s)
- Equipment to play music
- Films on folk dance
- Photographs of folk dancers
- Projector
- Recordings of folk dance music
- Resources on folk dance

## Advance Preparation

Invite folk dance groups and leaders to visit the class.

## Method

Jesus' words, known as the Great Commission recorded in Matthew 28:18-20, command us to share the good news of God's saving love with the whole world. One way to illustrate this story, as well as the message of the entire Bible, is through the use of folk dance. Folk dance is an interesting, involving way to build community while celebrating the uniqueness among cultures. Folk dance in its traditional recreational and ritualistic forms is generally considered anonymous in origin, and handed down from generation to generation in specific areas of the world. Many of the movements are symbolic and represent the actions of or reactions to people, nature, birds, and other animals.

Invite the students to learn a variety of folk dances from other countries. Begin by showing photographs of folk dancers or viewing a video of people dancing different steps. If a folk dance group or instructor has been invited to share with the students, introduce them to the class and ask the guests to perform. Invite the participants to learn folk dances from different cultures, such as:

- Caribbean Islands - Calypso
- Ethiopia - Eskista
- Greece – Trata
- Ireland – Jig
- Israel – Hora
- Mexico – La Cucaracha
- Moravia – Handkerchief dance
- Philippines – Liki
- Poland – Polka
- Scotland – Highland fling
- Spain – Paso Doble

Provide instructions and guide the group as they listen to the music and learn the steps.

Try a specific folk dance, the "Peace Prayer," which is a chant based on Isaiah 2:4. Its message, promoting world peace, is that people shall hammer their swords into plowshares, their spears into sickles, and that war shall end. Use a traditional Israeli grapevine step to accompany the words and music.

Gather the participants in a circle, in concentric circles, or in a line, and instruct them to move to the left. Tell the dancers to extend their hands along the adjoining person's arms, gripping wrists or elbows, or to extend their hands to opposite shoulders. Begin the music and the movements slowly and speed up as the dance progresses.

▶

Suggested movements include:

**Nation shall not**
*(Cross right foot behind left foot and bend knees. Step sideward on left foot.)*

**Lift sword**
*(Cross right foot in front of left foot.)*

**Against nation**
*(Continue the pattern throughout the rest of the dance.)*

To end the dance, draw the group into a circle and remind the participants to share the story of God's love with all people, regardless of their differences.

# Go with a Game

## Materials

► Bible(s)
► Equipment to play music
► Recording of waltz music

## Method

Select a game, like "Follow the Leader," and share a story through movement and music. Choose background music, perhaps the waltzes of Strauss or Tchaikovsky, since this rhythm encourages movement.

Gather the group and share a story, such as "David the Shepherd." Explain the process for the activity. Begin with the instructor as the "shepherd" and the participants as the "sheep." Start with simple warm-up movements for the students to follow, including:

► Bend side to side from the waist
► Heal-step right; Heal-step left
► Lift knees high
► Stretch hands over head
► Swing arms
► Touch toes.

Invite the participants to think of some movements. Continue the activity by marching around the room in different patterns. As the "sheep" become comfortable using movements, invite individuals to take a turn to be the "shepherd."

Think of additional stories to use for this format, such as the Old Testament accounts of Moses leading the Israelites through the wilderness or Joshua bringing the people into the promised land. Also review New Testament records of the feeding of the five thousand or the activity on Pentecost.

# Impart an Idea

## Materials

- ► Bible(s)
- ► Equipment to play music
- ► Props (optional)
- ► Recording of music without words

## Method

Creative movement, a form of improvisation, is the art of using natural body gestures to express emotions and to interpret ideas. Creative movement can be a physical as well as a spiritual experience.

Many times the most creative type of movement involves a person's free response to music. To prepare participants for this type of experience, the leader may offer suggestions such as "As you listen to this music, think about how it makes you feel" or "When you hear this music, how do you want to move your body?"

Refer to the Old Testament stories in which David, as well as his sister Miriam, used movement to express their praise to God. In Exodus 15:20-21, Miriam offered a lively dance to demonstrate her joy at the crossing of the Red Sea. In 2 Samuel 6:14, David danced before the Lord when the Ark of the Covenant was brought to Jerusalem. Re-enact these stories through a creative movement activity. Props, such as colored chiffon scarves or crepe paper streamers, can add to the enjoyment of creative movement. Frequently, these items encourage shy students to participate because attention is focused on the object rather than the person. Direct everyone in the group to select a scarf and to form a large circle. Encourage the participants to use the props, individually and collectively, to create gestures and movements that interpret the passage as it is read. Invite people to take turns dancing in the center of the circle and offering gestures for the group to try. If desired, play music without words in the background.

Many other Bible stories can be used to encourage learners to make believe with movement. Share the account of Creation, inviting participants to act out the events of each day, or tell the tale of Noah, asking students to pretend to be the animals on the ark. Encourage spontaneous movement to impart an idea.

# Interpret the Intent

## Materials

- Bible(s)
- Paper
- Pencils or pens
- Selected reading(s)

## Method

Start with a poem or a prayer, or a song or a speech, and interpret the intent through gesture. For example, add movement to the prayer of Saint Francis of Assisi, "Lord, Make Me an Instrument," and use it as a catalyst to explore ways in which each person can be a tool to share this message in today's world.

Read the words of the selection to the group.

Lord, make me an instrument of your
   peace.
Where there is hatred, let me so love,
Where there is injury, pardon,
Where there is darkness, light,
Where there is sadness, joy,
Where there is doubt, faith,
And where there is despair, hope.
O Divine Master,
Grant that I may not so much seek
To be consoled as to console,
To be understood as to understand,
To be loved as to love.
For it is in giving that we receive,
It is in pardoning that we are pardoned,
And it is in dying that we are born to
   eternal life.

Invite the group to add gestures and movements to express the meaning of the words. Assign each person or small group a phrase to interpret. Select someone to read the poem slowly and deliberately as the action takes place. Direct the group to change movements on the key phrases.

Suggest that the participants re-write Saint Francis' thoughts using their own words to form prayers related to modern-day situations. As a group, review each line of the poem. Name situations where there is hatred and suggest ways to show love. Or, consider circumstances in which there is sadness and offer ideas to bring joy. Distribute paper and pencils or pens and ask each individual to focus on a way in which he or she can be an instrument of peace in some of these situations. Share an example:

Lord, make me an instrument of your
   peace.
Where there is name calling,
let me bring kind words.
Where there is arguing,
let me bring problem solving.

Allow time for the group to write their prayers. Encourage the participants to interpret their new poems through movement.

# Modify the Movements

## Materials

► Bible(s)
► Equipment to play music (optional)
► Music to the "Macarena"

## Method

Select a popular dance, from the past or the present, and modify the movements and the words to proclaim a story. For example, adapt the "Macarena" and share Jesus' Summary of the Law, recorded in Matthew 22:37-39. The message might be:

Share God's love everywhere, everyway!
Share God's love with everyone,
   everyday!
Share God's love—Jesus showed us the
   way.
Yes! I can do it!

Set these words to the music of the once-popular dance fad, the "Macarena," and demonstrate the message through movement. For example:

**Share God's**
*(Extend right arm in front of body.)*

**Love**
*(Extend left arm in front of body.)*

**Everywhere**
*(Turn right arm with palm facing up.)*

**Everyway.**
*(Turn left arm with palm facing up.)*

**Share God's**
*(Bend right arm at elbow and touch left arm at elbow.)*

**Love**
*(Bend left arm at elbow and touch right arm at elbow.)*

**With everyone**
*(Extend right arm at side.)*

**Everyday.**
*(Extend left arm at side.)*

**Share God's**
*(Cross right arm over chest.)*

**Love**
*(Cross left arm over chest.)*

**Jesus**
*(Stretch right arm upward.)*

**Showed us the way.**
*(Stretch left arm upward.)*

**Yes!**
*(Clap hands overhead or snap fingers.)*

**I can do it!**
*(Improvise action such as clapping, turning, or wiggling.)*

# Pass the Peace

## Materials

- ► Accompaniment (Optional)
- ► Bible(s)
- ► Music for "Shalom Chaverim"

## Method

A ritual is a ceremonial, solemn rite that is used to communicate a specific message. "Passing the Peace" is a ritual that helps people share the story of God's love with others. Through movement, God's peace—"Shalom"—is exchanged. Involve the participants in an interpretive version of passing the peace by adding movements to the song "Shalom Chaverim." Gestures are suggested for each phrase.

To begin, have participants form pairs and stand facing each other. Guide the group as they learn the movements for each line of the song.

**Shalom, my friend**
*(Partners bring palms of one hand together as in a mirror image. Partner one uses right hand while partner two uses left hand.)*

**Shalom, my friend**
*(Repeat, using opposite hands.)*

**Shalom**
*(Keeping palms together, move hands up and outward in a circular motion until circle is completed.)*

**Shalom**
*(Each partner brings his or her palms together in front of the chest as in a greeting.)*

**May peace be with you**
*(Partners bow heads, hands, and upper bodies towards each other.)*

**May peace be with you**
*(Repeat action.)*

**Shalom**
*(Each person raises hands, repeating the circle movement.)*

**Shalom**
*(Cross hands over chest, touching fingertips to opposite shoulders.)*

# Sculpt the Story

## Materials

- ▶ Bible(s)
- ▶ Equipment to play music
- ▶ Recording of music
- ▶ Reference materials such as Bible concordances or Bible dictionaries

## Method

Scripture stories suggest actions and attitudes that help people show Christ's compassion and concern for individuals and groups in various situations. Involve the participants in gestural interpretation—body sculptures—to illustrate some of these important Bible passages.

Arrange the learners into small groups. Distribute paper, pens or pencils, and Bibles to each team. Ask the students to think of words that illustrate the ways in which Jesus wants us to treat others. Terms might include compassion, forgiveness, love, justice, and mercy. Direct the group to print one or more of these words on their papers. Provide additional research tools, such as Bible concordances or Bible dictionaries, and challenge each group to locate verses in Scripture that refer to these themes. Ask them to record ways that Jesus showed forgiveness, love, and justice to others. Give the students enough time to brainstorm words and to find Scripture references for some of them. Encourage the participants to share their passages with the entire group.

Once the students have completed this part of the activity, invite them to interpret several of the Bible passages through body gestures. Tell the participants to stand and to form a circle. Lead the students in using their bodies to sculpt the words. Hands, arms, and facial expressions are very important in this activity. Tell the group that a biblical theme will be stated and that each person or group, in turn, will take a pose to illustrate it. For example, if the leader says, "Sculpt compassion," the students might embrace one another. To illustrate healing, pupils may touch the head or hand of a neighbor. "Sculpt joy" may result in a simple dance movement.

Remind the learners that body language is more than a gestural activity. What people "say" with their bodies is just as important as what they "say" with their words. It is important to remember that compassion and concern can be shown to another with and without the use of words.

# Sign the Story

## Materials

- Bible(s)
- Book on sign language such as *The Joy of Signing: The Illustrated Guide for Mastering Sign Language and the Manual Alphabet.* (Riekehof, Lottie L. Gospel Publishing House, Second Edition, May, 1987.)

## Method

Sign language is a communication system using gestures that are interpreted visually. Many deaf people and those with a hearing loss use sign language as their primary means of conversation. In 1816, American educator Thomas Gallaudet traveled to Paris to study the French Method of deaf education. In 1817 he established the first U.S. school for the deaf and adapted the French signing method for use in the American classroom. The merger of French signs with movements in use by American deaf people formed what is now called American Sign Language. Like spoken languages, which use units of sounds to produce words, sign language uses units of form. These units are composed of four basic hand forms: hand shape, such as an open hand or closed fist; hand location, such as on the middle of the forehead or in front of the chest; hand movement, such as upward or downward; and hand orientation, such as the palm facing up or out. In sign language, units of form and meaning are typically combined simultaneously.

Since the hands of a person using sign language speak eloquently in silent motions, tell the story in this format. Begin by inviting someone familiar with the sign alphabet to teach it to the group. Practice over a period of several weeks. Then teach the signs for a psalm or song, illustrating the major words first. Gradually add the smaller, connecting words. When signing a song, make the movements rhythmic to match the tempo and mood of the music. Share the story through sign.

# Telling the Story through Drama

Drama is a powerful method to use to tell stories – including Bible stories. Whether a person is a member of an audience, a student reading a script for a classroom exercise, or a part of the cast or crew of a local production, many layers of learning take place during involvement in dramatic experiences.

Ten suggestions, offering different methods for using drama, are provided. They range from acting out skits and stories with various techniques and themes to preparing and presenting short scenes and situations on biblical concerns and concepts.

Regardless of the method used for conveying the information of the selected subject or script, use drama as a way to challenge the participants to learn Bible stories in engaging and entertaining ways.

# Add Some Action

## Materials

► Action story script
► Bible(s)

## Method

Start with any Bible story and add some action to tell it in a dramatic way. An "action story" includes gestures and movements to illustrate each line. Participants sit or stand facing the leader who tells the story and demonstrates the motions for the listeners. Words to be repeated can be written out on newsprint or on a chalkboard, or can simply be emphasized with the voice so that hearers understand the key words to repeat. Additional gestures and movements may be improvised by the group or by the leader. Select a Scripture passage and create an action story or try the one provided, which is based on Jesus' interaction with Zacchaeus, recorded in Luke 19:1-10.

**Zacchaeus: Called by Christ**
Luke 19:1-10

Jesus is coming!
*(Cup hands to mouth)*

Let's all go see!
*(Hold one hand over eyes and look around)*

Zacchaeus was short
*(Hold hand low to indicate short)*

so he climbed a tree!
*(Move hands in climbing motion)*

Soon Jesus walked by,
*(Walk in place)*

the crowd was so great.
*(Extend arms at sides)*

Jesus told Zacchaeus:
*(Place hand over eyes; look up)*

Come down now! Don't wait!
*(Motion come down)*

I'm going to come
*(Point to self)*

to your house today.
*(Point away from self)*

Go home; Get ready!
*(Point in distance)*

I'm on my way!
*(Walk in place)*

Zacchaeus I know
*(Point to head)*

all the ways you've sinned.
*(Shake head "no")*

So believe in God
*(Point up)*

and begin again.
*(Extend arm in gesture of invitation)*

Zacchaeus was sorry
*(Wipe tears from eyes)*

for the wrongs he'd done.
*(Shake head "no")*

He re-paid his debt
*(Gesture distributing money)*

to everyone.
*(Point to many people)*

He trusted Jesus
*(Fold hands in prayer)*

and made a new start.
*(Shake head "yes")*

Little Zacchaeus had a
*(Gesture short)*

big change of heart!
*(Place hands over heart)*

# Choose a Category

*Materials*

▸ Bible(s)
▸ Script(s)

*Method*

There are many possibilities for adapting and using drama scripts in storytelling activities. Select one dramatic method for the entire group to use, or enable the students to experiment with many techniques to tell the stories of the Bible. For example:

### Dramatization of Story
Act out a story while one person reads it from a script.

### First Person
Tell the character's story, as presented in the script, as if the speaker were the person.

### Formal Drama
Perform a full-scale production with memorized parts, costumes, lighting, sets, and so forth.

### Masks
Use masks to represent characters and act out the story as a script is read.

### Mime
Portray a story through the silent art of body movement.

### Pageant
Involve participants in a large project with creative possibilities for uniting many ages and groups within a congregation in a drama to commemorate a special occasion or festival in the church year.

### Play Reading
Invite students to read a script as a learning activity.

### Reader's Theater
Read from a script as a performance without memorizing the material. Costumes, props, and sets are generally not used.

### Recorder Drama
Act out a story while listening to a recording that has been prepared in advance.

### Tableau
Try a dramatic scene that is both silent and motionless. Players freeze in an interesting pose for a few minutes as interpretation of the scene is offered through message or music.

# Compose Some Conversation

## Materials

- Bible(s)
- Pencils or pens
- Paper

## Method

Choose a Scripture passage, write an original script, and act out the story.

Start by selecting a biblical theme that will be the basis of the performance. Since the story needs to have a beginning, a middle, and an end—also called Acts I, II, and III—decide on the action that takes place in each scene and the characters that are needed in each section. In Act One, the beginning, establish the time and place. Introduce the main character and his or her relationship to the other personalities. Set up the conflict. During Act Two, the middle, highlight the series of events that move towards the climax, or confrontation, of the conflict. In the end, Act Three, resolve the conflict in a believable way.

Pass out paper and pencils and allow time for the pupils to outline each scene and to write dialogue between the characters. Offer assistance and encouragement where needed. Determine costumes, props, and scenery that could be used to enhance the story.

Arrange to present some or all of the dramas for other classes or groups.

# Experience an Event

## Materials

- Bible(s)
- Information on local and regional productions
- Projection equipment
- Recording of a biblical drama
- Screen

## Method

Countless plays that communicate a biblical concept, depict a religious theme, or portray a Scripture story have been written in the past, and are being produced in the present. More are always in the process of being penned, prepared, and performed. Help participants become aware of opportunities to explore and experience biblical subjects through drama. For example, attend a performance. Arrange for an outing to a production such as a pageant at a local church, a musical at a community theater, or a Passion play at a summer camp. Discuss the content of the show before and after the event. If it is not possible to attend an actual performance, watch a production that has been recorded.

# Improvise the Information

## Materials

- ► Bible(s)
- ► Magazines
- ► Newspapers

## Method

Improvise is a word that means to compose or to perform without preparation; to make or do with whatever is at hand. In drama, an improvisation might take place in response to hearing or reading a Scripture passage or a story. It could also occur as a reaction to handling an object, listening to music, participating in a conversation, or seeing a picture.

"Newspaper drama" is an interesting method to use to create improvisation. This is an especially relevant way to help people make the connection between biblical concepts and current events.

Arrange the participants into small groups. Provide each team with a stack of current magazines and newspapers. Invite each group to find and to agree on one article that pertains to the selected Scripture passage, for example a justice issue such as the Jubilee, recorded in Leviticus 25. Explain that the groups will review their articles and will improvise and act out the situations. Each person must have a part to play.

Give the teams ten to 15 minutes to find the articles and to prepare the skits. Then invite the groups to take turns presenting their dramas for the entire assembly. After everyone has shared their improvisations, discuss the scenes and the justice concerns and concepts that they illustrate. Some teams might even want to improvise possible solutions to the suggested scenarios.

# Interview for Information

## Materials

► Bible(s)
► Paper
► Pencils or pens

## Method

Use drama to help participants apply Scripture stories to modern day situations. For example, pose a question such as "How do we show God's love to others?" Then conduct a series of interviews to discover some answers. Challenge the group to present the information in a TV news show format.

Begin the project by reading a Scripture passage such as Matthew 25:37-40:

> Lord, when was it that we saw you hungry and gave you food, or thirsty and gave you something to drink? And when was it that we saw you a stranger and welcomed you, or naked and gave you clothing? And when was it that we saw you sick or in prison and visited you? Truly I tell you, just as you did it to one of the least of these who are members of my family, you did it to me.

Discuss ways that people today share God's love with those who are hungry, thirsty, strangers, poor, sick, and imprisoned.

Invite the participants to interview a variety of people to obtain answers to this question. Then challenge the group to present the information they gather in the format of a TV news show.

Assign one or more participants to each theme, such as "How is God's love shared with the hungry?" or "How do people today show God's love to the sick?" Or, give each learner a source to interview such as a member of the family, a person in the congregation, a teacher in the school, or an official in the community.

Once the information has been collected, discuss the process for presenting it in a TV news show format. Take turns having one or several students be the host or anchor team, and let the others be the people who are interviewed or who report their findings. Give the students the opportunity to write short statements and to practice and present the program.

# Perform with Props

## Materials

- Bible(s)
- Boxes
- Costume pieces such as accessories, blouses, hats, pants, shirts, shoes, and skirts
- Props

## Advance Preparation

Prepare a costume/prop box for each team.

## Method

Offer costumes or props and create instant drama! Invite the students to participate in short skits on the selected theme, such as the calling of the disciples. Arrange the players into groups of equal size. Explain that one person in each group will play the role of Jesus. Remaining students may play the parts of the disciples, as well as people associated with them such as co-workers, family, and friends.

Distribute a box to each team. Inform the groups that they will go to separate areas of the room and prepare a skit using the costume pieces and/or objects and props in the box they received. Tell the students that the objects may or may not be used for their normal function; however, each object must be included in the skit and each person must participate in the play. Note that the skits are to run approximately two to three minutes and that they may be presented verbally, with words, or non-verbally, without words. Allow preparation time.

After the skits are planned and rehearsed, invite the groups to return and to take turns presenting them. After the short dramas, converse with the students about differences and similarities in the interpretation of the skits.

# Practice the Parts

## Materials

► Bible(s)
► Paper
► Pencils or pens
► Script for Choral Reading

## Method

Choral reading is a type of drama in which lines are read or recited in parts and in unison under the direction of a leader. Blending words, phrases, and sentences to interpret a passage or a story creates drama. Share Scripture through choral reading.

Invite the group to find Psalm 96 in their Bibles. Read the passage in unison. Invite the participants to learn it or to listen to it as a choral reading. Explain that in this type of drama high or low voices, solos, and group combinations give interpretation to each phrase or sentence of a piece of writing. If people have already prepared the script, have them present it for the class. If the entire group will participate in the project, assign parts and practice the reading. Present the choral reading for various church school classes or as part of a worship service.

Psalm 96 Choral Reading Script (NRSV)

UNISON:  O sing to the Lord
a new song;

SOLO ONE:  sing to the Lord,
all the earth.

SOLO TWO:  Sing to the Lord;
bless his name.

FEMALES:  tell of his salvation
from day to day.

SOLO THREE:  Declare His glory
among the nations,

MALES:  his marvelous works
among all the peoples.

UNISON:  For great is the Lord,
and greatly to be praised;
He is to be revered
above all gods.

SOLO ONE:  For all the gods of
the peoples are idols,

SOLO TWO:  but the Lord
made the heavens.

FEMALES:  Honor and majesty
are before him;

MALES:  strength and beauty
are in his sanctuary.

SOLO THREE:  Ascribe to the Lord,

SOLO FOUR:  O families of the peoples,

SOLO ONE:  Ascribe to the Lord glory

SOLO TWO:  and strength.

FEMALES:  Ascribe to the Lord
the glory due his name;

MALES:  bring an offering
and come into his courts.

UNISON:  Worship the Lord
in holy splendor;

SOLO THREE:  tremble before him,
all the earth.

SOLO FOUR:  Say among the nations,
"The Lord is king!"

FEMALES:  The world is firmly
established,

MALES:  It shall never be moved;

| | |
|---|---|
| UNISON: | He will judge the peoples with equity. |
| SOLO ONE: | Let the heavens be glad, |
| SOLO TWO: | and let the earth rejoice; |
| SOLO THREE: | Let the sea roar, |
| SOLO FOUR: | And all that fills it; |
| SOLOS ONE & TWO: | Let the field exalt, |
| SOLOS THREE & FOUR: | And everything in it. |
| FEMALES: | Then shall all the trees of the forest sing for joy; |
| MALES: | before the Lord; |
| SOLO ONE: | For he is coming, |
| SOLO TWO: | For he is coming to judge the earth. |
| UNISON: | He will judge the world with righteousness and the peoples with his truth. |

# Re-create a Role

## Materials

► Bible(s)

## Method

Role-play, a dramatic method, is intended to enable a person to experience the emotions of another individual. Role-play helps a person step into a situation to experience how someone in that position or those circumstances might have acted or felt.

Choose one of the "family" stories in the Bible and role-play one or more of the interactive scenes between parents and children. Examples include the Old Testament account of father Isaac, mother Rebekah, and children Esau and Jacob or the New Testament narrative of the family members of the story of the Prodigal Son.

Review the steps in the role-play process and try this drama technique in classes and groups.

**Step One**
Read the Bible passage or the story together.

**Step Two**
Decide on roles and ask for volunteers.

**Step Three**
Review the situation.

**Step Four**
Clarify roles rather than offering suggestions for playing the character.

**Step Five**
Spontaneously enact the situation. Ask certain members of the group to observe a specific character.

**Step Six**
Stop the action after several minutes, or following the climax, or as players run out of dialog.

**Step Seven**
Discuss the situation. Help group members attempt to understand how the people in the scene might have felt and why they may have acted as they did. Guide the discussion so that judgments will not be given on the acting skill of the participants. Remember that the purpose of role-play is to experience and to observe a situation first-hand, not to critique a dramatic production.

**Step Eight**
Repeat the scene with new people playing the roles, or choose a new situation to illustrate through this drama technique.

# Script the Scripture

## Materials

► Bible(s)
► Paper
► Pencils or pens

## Method

Create an easy script from the words of a Scripture passage by following four simple steps. In a "Scripture script" format, the goal is to arrange the Bible verses into character parts so that the passage will be more understandable to those hearing it. The object is not to embellish the text and to add details that are not suggested, but to adhere as closely as possible to the words of the Bible.

### Step One
Identify the characters in the passage and make a list of these people.

### Step Two
Find all of the quotes in the passage. Match a character to each of them. Letter the person's name on the left side of a paper, and write the words of the quote next to it. Try to break long passages into several parts.

### Step Three
Write lines for any other portion of the passage that could be assigned to a specific person.

### Step Four
Add a narrator, or several, to provide information between the speaking parts.

A sample script based on Luke 2:1-20, the Christmas story, is provided. Take turns playing the parts: Narrator, Caesar Augustus, Joseph, Mary, Angels, and Shepherds.

Drape strips of fabric over the actors' and actresses' heads and shoulders, if desired, to create simple costumes.

## Sample Scripture Story Script
*Based on Luke 2:1-20*

CAESAR AUGUSTUS: **A census must be taken of the entire Roman world. Everyone must go to his or her own town to register.**

JOSEPH: **Mary, we must go from Nazareth to Bethlehem, because I am of the house and line of David.**

MARY: **It will be a long journey for me since my baby is due to be born very soon.**

NARRATOR: **Upon arriving in Bethlehem, Joseph and Mary discovered that there was no room for them in the inn.**

JOSEPH: **We will stay in the stable where the cattle are kept.**

NARRATOR: **While they were there, the time came for the baby to be born, and Mary gave birth to her firstborn, a son.**

MARY: **Let us wrap the baby in cloths to keep Him warm.**

JOSEPH: **We can place Him in the manger.**

NARRATOR: **There were shepherds living out in the fields nearby, keeping watch over their flocks.**

SHEPHERD ONE: **One night, an angel of the Lord appeared to us, and the glory of the Lord shone around us, and we were terrified.**

ANGEL: **Do not be afraid, I bring you good news of great joy that will be for all the people. Today in the town of David a Savior has been born to you; He is Christ the Lord. This will be a sign to you: You will find a baby wrapped in cloths and lying in a manger.**

SHEPHERD TWO: **A great company of the heavenly host appeared with the angel, praising God and saying:**

ANGELS: **Glory to God in the highest, and on earth peace to those on whom God's favor rests.**

NARRATOR: **When the angels returned to heaven, the shepherds said to one another:**

SHEPHERD ONE: **Let's go to Bethlehem and see this thing that has happened, which the Lord has told us about.**

SHEPHERD TWO: **After we worshipped the baby, we spread the word concerning what had been told to us about this child.**

SHEPHERD TWO: **All who heard it were amazed at what we said to them.**

MARY: **I will treasure all of these things and ponder them in my heart.**

NARRATOR: **The shepherds returned, glorifying and praising God for all that they had heard and seen, which were just as they had been told.**

# Telling the Story through Games

People of all ages and abilities can enjoy and learn from games. Games are a great way to mix people, and in the process, to strengthen friendships and relationships. The current emphasis in game playing is on cooperation rather than competition. When people work together, instead of against each other, the elements of advantage and the fear of being eliminated are removed. Each player tends to feel good about himself or herself and these feelings are shared with other participants.

Ten games, with many variations on formats, are suggested as storytelling tools. Most of these games may be led by people with no prior experience and no particular expertise. They do not require expensive equipment or time consuming preparation. Use any or all of these ideas to tell the story in interactive ways.

# Brief with Bingo

## Materials

- Bible(s)
- Chalkboard and chalk or newsprint and markers
- Containers
- Copier or duplicating equipment
- Game markers such as buttons, paper squares, or pennies
- Paper
- Pencils or pens
- Ruler(s)

## Advance Preparation

Divide a piece of 8 ½" x 11" paper into twenty-five squares to form a grid five squares by five squares.

Duplicate a Bingo sheet for each participant.

## Method

Create a game of "Bingo" to help participants learn facts and terms associated with a story.

Begin by brainstorming twenty-five words related to the theme. Print the list on a chalkboard or on a piece of newsprint. Discuss each idea as it is mentioned. Twenty-five possibilities for the story of Noah include:

- Altar
- Animals
- Ark
- Daughters-in-law
- Disobedience
- Door
- Dove
- Flood
- God
- Gopher Wood
- Ham
- Japheth
- Neighbors
- Noah
- Obedience
- Olive Branch
- Rain
- Rainbow
- Raven
- Shem
- Sin
- Thanks
- Two
- Water
- Wife

Supplement the participant's ideas with items from this list.

Distribute copies of the blank Bingo board and pencils or pens to all participants. Instruct the group to print one word or phrase in each square as it is read from the list they complied. Explain that each participant should put the words in his or her own order, so that each Bingo game is unique. As the students print words on their game boards, the leader should write the word or phrase on a separate small slip of paper. Deposit the slips into a container from which they will be drawn randomly as play takes place. When all participants are ready, place game markers within sharing distance of each person. Play begins when the leader draws a word out of the container and reads it aloud. Each player uses a game marker to cover the place containing that word or phrase on his or her card. Play continues until one person has five spaces covered in a row, which could be diagonally, horizontally, or vertically. Repeat the game as long as players show interest or until everyone "Bingos" at the same time.

# Concentrate on Content

## Materials

► Bible(s)

► Colored pencils, crayons, or markers

► Construction paper

► Glue

► Magazines

► Scissors

## Method

Play a game of Concentration to emphasize the content of a Scripture story. Select scenes, situations, or symbols related to the passage and illustrate the ideas onto the game pieces for the activity. If the participants are to make the parts, distribute two identical pieces of paper to each person. Offer supplies such as colored pencils, crayons, or markers as well as glue, magazines, and scissors. Tell the learners to draw two identical pictures or to find two of the same photo, putting one on each sheet of paper. Make sure that one side of each paper is left blank. Collect the pieces from each person.

Shuffle the cards and spread them out, picture side down, in a tiled pattern on the floor or on a table. If there are a large number of participants, prepare two or more games. However, be sure to keep the pairs together within a given game. Instruct the players to take turns exposing the cards and attempting to make matches. Each player may turn two cards over during his or her turn. If the illustrations match, ask the student to state the picture's connection to the story.

If they do not match, return the cards to a face down position. The next person may attempt to make a match by turning over two cards. Play continues until all pairs have been uncovered. When the game is over, use the pictures as a bulletin board display or combine the papers to create two books that may be shared with other people.

Try a variation of a traditional "Concentration" game. Supplies include ten duplicate sets of illustrations related to the story, as well as clear self-adhesive paper, construction paper, glue, markers, poster board, and scissors. To make the game pieces, select ten sets of illustrations. Glue one picture from each set of illustrations to construction paper to make it firm. Trim the ten pieces to make them the same size. For durability, cover the pictures with clear self-adhesive paper. To prepare the game board, select a piece of poster board large enough to hold all twenty pieces, allowing for spaces in between them. With a marker, outline spaces for twenty pictures - four rows of five. On the second and fourth rows, glue one set of ten pictures in the spaces.

For a one-player game, stack the individual picture cards in front of the person and ask him or her to match them with the cards glued on the board. For two players, stack the ten cards face down between the players. Each, in turn, selects a card, looks at the picture, and matches it with one on the board. It is then placed in the appropriate space on the poster. Play continues until the players have matched all the spaces on the board. To increase learning, instruct each player to explain the illustration's connection to the story.

# Cooperate in Class

## Materials

- Bible(s)
- Books of cooperative games
- Supplies for games

## Method

Introduce participants to a variety of theme-related cooperative games and use them during class periods or recreation time. Cooperative, rather than competitive, games help students learn to play and to work together to achieve common goals.

Review books of cooperative games, such as:

***The Cooperative Sports and Games Book.*** Orlick, Tom. New York: Pantheon Books, 1978.

Book with a wealth of activities emphasizing cooperative approaches to playing games and sports.

***More New Games and Playful Ideas from the New Games Foundation.*** Fluegelman, Andrew, Editor. San Francisco, CA: The Headlands Press, 1981.

Games for two, a dozen, two dozen, and many more people.

***The New Games Book: Play Hard, Play Fair, Nobody Hurt.*** Fluegelman, Andrew, Editor. San Francisco, CA: The Headlands Press, 1976.

Sixty new games, together with many photographs, to encourage creativity and cooperation.

***Play Fair: Everybody's Guide to Noncompetitive Play.*** Weinstein, Matt and Joel Goodman. San Luis Obispo, CA: Impact Publishers, 1980.

An introduction to the area of play as well as chapters on cooperative games including mixers, energizers, mind games, leadership training games, and endings.

***Everyone Wins!: Cooperative Games and Activities.*** Luvmour, Josette and Sambhava Luvmour. Gabriola Island, BC: New Society Publishers, 2007.

Over 150 cooperative games and activities in an updated edition of this Parent Choice Award-winner.

Use group-building activities to review Bible stories that emphasize cooperation. An Old Testament example would be the Israelite's escape from their slavery in Egypt and a New Testament account could be Paul's letters to the early churches.

In addition to using new games, adapt competitive game formats to a cooperative game emphasis. For example, play "Musical Chairs" in a way in which people are included rather than excluded. Set up chairs in the center of the room, one for each participant. Place the chairs in a circle, facing toward or away from each other, or line them up in a row, facing alternate directions. With a large group, players may arrange the chairs two deep, back to back. Play background music and direct the participants to walk around the chairs until the music stops. At that point tell everyone to find a seat. Eliminate a chair each time the music stops, but allow all participants to continue to play the game. Double up on chairs until all players share one seat at the end.

# Guide with a Game

## Materials

- ▶ Bible(s)
- ▶ Dice
- ▶ Index cards
- ▶ Markers
- ▶ Pens
- ▶ Playing pieces
- ▶ Poster board

## Advance Preparation

- ▶ Prepare the game board.
- ▶ Select themes associated with a story, such as passages, places, and people. Print each theme word on one side of several index cards.
- ▶ Write a theme-related question on each card. Sample questions based on people in the story of Joseph might include "What was the name of Joseph's father?" or "Name Joseph's youngest brother." Possible questions for the places category could be "Where did the brothers put Joseph?" or "Name the country Joseph helped rule." Place the cards on the game board.

## Method

Make and use a board game format to help participants learn information about a lesson. To construct the game board, select a full piece of poster board. Draw a large horseshoe shape on the sheet, positioned horizontally or vertically. Divide the shape into twenty squares. Label the first square "Start" and the last square "End" or "Finish." Write the theme-related words—those that correspond with the index card headings—on the squares, staggering them throughout the game board. For example, two squares from "Start" print the word "People." Three squares from "People" letter the word "Places," and so forth. Do this until all headings are used, repeating them a number of times. In addition, print directions such as "Move Ahead One Space," "Go Back Two Squares," or "Challenge Someone to Answer a Question" in some of the squares.

To play the game, invite each student to select a playing piece and to place it on the square marked "Start." Direct the players, in turn, to throw one die and to move the number of spaces indicated on the piece. As the students land on the squares, they must follow the directions written in the spaces. If they land on a "Theme" they must select a corresponding card, read the question, and offer an answer. If the information is correct, the player may take another turn. The first player to reach the "End" square wins. Repeat the game as long as the students are interested in playing it.

# Hold a Hunt

## Materials

- Bible(s)
- Pens
- Scavenger hunt lists

## Advance Preparation

Prepare scavenger hunt lists.

## Method

In a scavenger hunt, a popular party game, individuals or teams are given a list of items to find and a designated time and area in which to locate them. This popular technique is a good way to help participants learn more about the concepts and content of a story.

For example, try a scavenger hunt based on the account of Paul's missionary journeys. Sample items on the list could include:

- Bible story book containing an account of Paul's journeys
- Boat (any size!)
- Book on the life of Paul
- Brochure from a local mission
- Bulletin listing the names of missionaries supported by a congregation
- Item from Greece
- Letter from a missionary
- Map of Turkey
- Newsletter from a church named "St. Paul's"
- Picture of Paul, the New Testament missionary
- Pita bread
- Postcard from a site Paul visited
- Sandals.

Tell the learners that they will go on a scavenger hunt to locate items that are related to a story. Assign the individuals to teams, and if necessary, provide a chaperone or a driver for each group. Indicate the procedure for the game. It could be played in the church building by moving from room to room to look for resources. It could also be held in the community by going from house-to-house, or to a public facility such as a mall, to find the objects. Distribute the scavenger hunt lists and review them together so the learners understand what they are being asked to find. Review the guidelines, such as time limit, location boundaries, safety issues, and so forth, and answer any questions that will clarify the procedure.

When the groups have finished the scavenger hunt, compare items so everyone can become more aware of the content of the story. Award prizes to the team that located the most items, the people who offered a unique contribution, or to everyone who participated in the game.

# Introduce with Ice-breakers

## Materials

▶ Bible(s)
▶ Supplies for the activity

## Method

Help participants learn each other's names—as well as information about a story—by using this easy, engaging exercise.

For young participants, call one person's name and toss a beanbag to him or her. Ask the person to share one idea from the selected story. That person then calls a name and tosses the beanbag to another student. Play continues in this manner until everyone has had a turn, or until the names are learned.

For older players, have one person begin by stating his or her name and adding one idea from a Bible story. The next person repeats this information and adds his or her own name and statement.

For example, using the life of David as the Bible story the first player might say, "My name is Paul and David was a shepherd." The second person could continue with, "This is Paul and he said David was a shepherd. I am Maddox and I remember that David was the youngest in his family." The third participant might add, "Paul said David was a shepherd, Maddox remembered David was the youngest in his family. I am Liz and David had a friend named Jonathan."

As play continues, and as the list grows longer, encourage and enable the pupils to cooperate to remember the information.

# Link the Lesson

## Materials

- Bible(s)
- Cellophane tape or stapler and staples
- Construction paper
- Markers
- Paper cutter or scissors

## Advance Preparation

Cut sheets of construction paper into 1" strips.

Select vocabulary words from the story and letter each of them on a separate paper. On separate strips, print definitions or descriptions of these words.

## Method

Link the lesson by using a matching game and creating a paper chain. Tell the group that each person will receive a strip of construction paper. Half of the papers have vocabulary words associated with the story. The other half have phrases or sentences that are definitions or descriptions related to each word. The task is to connect the two parts. When a match is made, the two players staple or tape their strips to form links.

Pass out the construction paper pieces that were prepared in advance. Instruct the players to move around the room asking questions of each another, and locating the matching words and phrases. When everyone has made a match, go around the group asking one partner to read the word and the other to state the definition or description. Supply additional information about the meaning of the terms, as needed. As each set of players completes a turn, have them add their links to the chain, using blank strips to join the pieces.

# Prepare Some Papers

## Materials

- ► Bible(s)
- ► Computer
- ► Copier or duplicating equipment
- ► Paper
- ► Pencils or pens
- ► Printer
- ► Resource materials

## Method

Design and use paper and pencil games as children's bulletins, classroom activities, or take-home sheets. Duplicate a copy for each participant. Try any or all of the following formats in individual or group settings.

### Alphabet Challenge

Print the alphabet down the left side of the paper. Challenge players to write a word associated with the theme for every letter from A-Z. A clue may be written by each line to offer a hint for the participants.

### Category Columns

Write a theme-related heading across the top of a piece of paper. Down the left side, list five categories such as animal, boy's name, girl's name, flower, and food. Fill in the columns with names and words that begin with the letters of the heading.

### Code

Prepare a code for every letter of the alphabet. Print a theme-related Scripture verse in the code and have the players decipher it.

### Connect the Dots

Form the outline of a theme-related symbol with dots. Place a number by each one and have the players connect the dots to identify the picture.

### Crossword Puzzles

Create a crossword puzzle using words related to the theme.

### Matching

In random order, prepare two columns of ten items each. The first column might list Scripture references and the second would be the verses. Or, the first column could be a name and the second would provide information about the person, place, or thing.

### Scrambled Words

Scramble familiar words associated with the theme. Ask players to unscramble them.

### Tic Tac Toe

Compile a list of questions related to the Scripture story. Ask one and, if a correct answer is given, allow that player to make an "X" or an "O" in any square. Conclude the game when one person has three marks in any direction.

### Who am I?

Write short sentences describing characters in the story and ask players to name them.

### Word Find

Write a phrase, such as the name of the story, and challenge players to see how many words they can make from the letters.

### Word Pictures

Make word pictures by writing the letters of a word in random order to form a shape. Challenge players to write the answer to each picture puzzle.

### Word Search

Create a word search and ask the participants to circle the hidden terms. Words may be hidden horizontally, vertically, or diagonally, forward or backward.

# Quiz with Questions

## Materials

► Bible(s)
► Supplies for the activity

## Method

It is often important to separate fact from fiction when teaching or telling a Bible story, the life of a saint, the sacraments, or a faith topic. Try one or more of the game formats that involve the use of questions. Two possibilities include:

### Fact/Fiction Cards

Cover a shoe box with construction paper. Prepare index cards with true and false statements related to the story. Write one statement on each card. Play a "true or false" game to help participants separate some of the myths and the realities related to the story. Place the playing cards in the decorated shoe box. Gather the group in a circle and invite each person, in turn, to draw a card from the box. Tell the individual to read the statement and to indicate whether it is true or false. Encourage cooperation rather than competition, and urge the group members to help one another come up with the right answer. Share correct information for each of the false statements. Display the true and the false statements on separate posters.

Another way to play the game is to have each participant draw a card from the box. Instruct the players to read their sentences silently. Tell the people who think that they have true statements to go to one side of the room and those who feel that they have false information to go to the other side of the room. Take turns having each side read their statements. Determine whether the information is actually true or false and adjust the sides accordingly.

Regardless of the way in which the game is played, help the students to know what is true and what is not true with regard to the selected story.

### Jeopardy

In a game of Jeopardy an answer is revealed to an individual or a group and the question must be supplied. In advance, prepare the game board. Print three to five categories at the top of a chalkboard or a piece of poster board. Compose five questions for each category and print them on separate index cards. In order of difficulty, write the point value—10, 20, 30, 40, or 50—on the other side of each card. Compile corresponding questions on a separate piece of paper.

To play the game, explain the game board. Invite the first individual or team to select a category and a point value. After the leader reads the answer, the player(s) have one minute to state the question. If they provide the correct question, they will be given the points. If they cannot come up with the question, the other player or team may attempt it. Rotate teams after each question. The game ends when all "answers" are revealed or when a predetermined number of points are reached. Discuss any questions and answers that need clarification.

# Run a Relay

## Materials

► Bible(s)
► Supplies for the activity

## Method

Run a relay to review a story in a unique way. A relay game is a type of race that is generally played in a gym or social hall, a large room, or outdoors. Leaders and players establish a race course with start and finish lines. A relay course may be a circle or a long straight line. The course may also go from a beginning mark to a midpoint, then back to the starting place. In this type of race, all team members line up single file behind the start line. Every runner goes to the midpoint to perform an action and returns to the start line to pass a "go" signal to the next person on the team. Generally, the first team to have all of its players finish the course is the winner.

Example of "Relay Reviews" could include having a box of biblical costumes at the midpoint and directing players to run to the box, name a character from the story, put on and take off a costume, and go back to the starting point. Another option might be to have a box of objects related to the story at the halfway point. Each player, in turn, would run to the midpoint, select an object, state its connection to the story, and run to the end.

# Telling the Story through Music

Learn a song about an Old Testament person. Try an instrument that was mentioned in the Bible. Listen to a song to introduce a lesson. Attend a performance of a children's choir from another country. Write new words to an old tune to express an idea. These are just some of the ways in which music can be used to tell a story.

From the songs of Miriam and Mary, the praise of the Psalmists and Paul, to the hymns of the host of angels in Bethlehem and the hundreds of thousands of saints in heaven, the use of music is recorded throughout Scripture as a way to help people express a wide range of human feelings. In biblical times, as well as today, music plays a part at family gatherings and celebrations (Genesis 31:27; Luke 15:25), accompanies work (Isaiah 16:10; Jeremiah 48:33; Numbers 21:17), and finds uses in military strategies and victory celebrations (Exodus 32:17-18; Joshua 6:4-20; Judges

7:18-10; Judges 11:34-35; 1 Samuel 18:6-7). Music has always been part of worship (1 Chronicles 15:16; 23:5; 25:6-7; 2 Chronicles 5:11-14; Ezra 2:65; Nehemiah 12:27-43), and of mourning and lament (2 Samuel 1:17-18; 2 Chronicles 35:25; Matthew 9:23). Refer to concordances and Bible reference books for additional information about the uses of music throughout Scripture.

Today music is used extensively in the worship, education, outreach, and nurture ministries of congregations. It is an art form and a teaching tool which is familiar to both the educator and the pupil. Since it is a participatory learning activity, it is a good method to use to involve people in the storytelling process.

Ten ideas for telling the story through music are provided. They include many themes and techniques. Use them as springboards for telling stories in various situations and settings.

# Chant a Chapter

## Materials

► Bible(s)

## Method

Select a favorite Psalm and sing it antiphonally. Explain that antiphonal means that a hymn or Psalm is sung in responsive, alternating parts. This was often the way people in Bible times sang their songs as they worshipped in the synagogue. A well-known song that is commonly sung antiphonally is "Hallelu, Praise Ye the Lord." One group sings "Hallelu" while the other group responds "Praise Ye the Lord."

After the Psalm is selected, and the words and music are reviewed, divide the singers into two groups. One group will sing a phrase and then the second group will sing a line. Praise God by singing a Psalm antiphonally.

# Create a Concert

## Materials

► Bible(s)
► Hymnals

## Method

Explore a theme, such as missions, through music. Provide a variety of hymnbooks and invite the group to search through them for songs which convey mission messages. Challenge each church school class to learn at least one song. Suggest that all of the selections be combined and that a concert for the congregation and the community be given. Feature the music of various ethnic groups and focus on themes such as love and justice at this special event. Incorporate opportunities for the audience to participate, too. Highlight the cause of missions and take an offering for a specific project.

# Harmonize for the Holidays

## Materials

- ▶ Bible(s)
- ▶ Glue or glue sticks
- ▶ Hymnal(s)
- ▶ Manila file folders or poster board
- ▶ Pens
- ▶ Pictures of Christmas scenes
- ▶ Scissors

## Method

Provide a creative way to sing the story of Christmas. In advance, select large, colorful pictures which depict holiday themes. Choose one picture for each group of five participants. Cut a piece of poster board or a manila file folder to fit the picture and glue the photo to it to add strength and rigidity. Cut each picture into five puzzle pieces. On the back of the five pieces from one picture, write the name of a familiar seasonal song. Suggestions include using "Joy to The World," "Silent Night," and "O Come All Ye Faithful." Repeat this process with a different song for each picture. Mix up all the puzzle pieces.

Randomly distribute one puzzle piece to each person. Inform the participants that they will be singing the songs written on their puzzle pieces while moving around the room trying to locate others who are singing the same song. If an individual does not know the song, instruct him or her to say the title while looking for the other partners. When the five "singers" find each other, have them form a group and complete the puzzle. If the students do not know each other, each should introduce him or herself.

After the instructions are given, invite each person to begin singing and searching. After all the groups are formed, sing or learn the songs together as a way of celebrating the Christmas story and season. Try this method for other holidays, too.

# Invent Some Instruments

## Materials

- ▶ Bible(s)
- ▶ Paper
- ▶ Pencils or pens
- ▶ Pictures of Bible times instruments (optional)

## Method

In biblical, as well as historic and modern times, a variety of musical instruments have been used to praise God. Psalm 150 is an exciting witness to the different types of instruments used in early worship experiences. Although this Psalm could be read in twenty seconds, if each instrument mentioned in it was played, it could last twenty minutes, or even two hours! Read Psalm 150 to or with the participants. Use an activity to explore the variety of musical instruments mentioned in the Bible.

Distribute pieces of paper on which the Scripture references related to instruments have been written. Invite individuals or small groups to look up each verse and to name the instrument described in it. Show examples or pictures, if possible, and offer additional information about the devises and their uses during Bible times. References to use include:

### Psalm 150:5 - Castanets
Two chestnuts attached to the fingers and beaten together to make music

### Psalm 98:6; Daniel 3:5,7,10,15 - Coronet
Instrument made from hollow, curved animal horns, and later from metal

### 2 Samuel 6:5; Psalm 150:5; 1 Corinthians 13:1 - Cymbals
Two concave plates of brass clanged together

### Exodus 15:20; Judges 11:34; Psalm 68:25; Psalm 81:2; 1 Chronicles 13:8 - Drum (also called timbrel, tambour, tambourine)
Wooden hoop with skin pulled across the frame

### Daniel 3:5,10,15 - Dulcimer
Resonance box with strings stretched across it played with small hammers

### Judges 5:16; Daniel 3:5 - Flute
Straight pipe with holes

### Genesis 4:21; 1 Samuel 16:16 - Harp
Wooden frame with strings

### 1 Samuel 16:23 - Lyre
Five or more strings stretched across a rectangular frame, similar to a harp

### Genesis 4:21; Job 21:12; Psalm 150:4 - Organ
Reed instrument made of wood, ivory, or bone, similar to an oboe

### 1 Samuel 10:5; 2 Chronicles 5:12; Psalm 71:22 - Psaltery
Bottle shaped stringed instrument, similar to a harp

### Daniel 3:5,7,10,15 - Sackbut
Portable, harp-like instrument tied to the player's waist

### Numbers 10:1-10; Judges 7:16-23; Matthew 24:31; 1 Corinthians 15:52; 1 Thessalonians 4:16; Revelation 8:2 - Trumpet
Instrument made from the horn of a ram or goat, and occasionally from silver

## Psalm 33:2; Psalm 144:9 - Zither
Ten stringed instrument, similar to the harp

Continue the activity by making rhythm instruments from recyclable items. Provide a variety of materials for the participants to use and demonstrate a number of methods for making the objects. Suggestions include:

## Chimes
Tie nails on various lengths of string, attach the strings to a coat hanger, and strike the nails with a larger nail to devise chimes.

## Drums
Form drums from coffee cans with plastic lids, and use dowel rods as the sticks.

## Scrapers
Cover blocks of wood, or egg cartons, with sandpaper and rub two of them together as scrapers

## Shakers
Fill empty plastic laundry bottles with pebbles to create shakers.

## Tambourine
Design a tambourine by punching holes around the edge of an aluminum pie plate and attaching bells to the holes with pipe cleaners.

Read Psalm 150 again and experiment with the different rhythm instruments to produce sounds of praise to God.

# Note the New Testament

## Materials

► Bible(s)
► Chalk or markers
► Chalkboard or newsprint
► Hymnals
► Paper
► Pencils or pens

## Method

Emphasize New Testament stories in which music is mentioned by engaging the participants in a game of "Win, Lose, or Draw." On slips of paper, write Scripture references and brief descriptions of several uses of music in the New Testament. Passages to use include:

**Matthew 26:30; Mark 14:26**
Song at the conclusion of the Last Supper

**Luke 1:46-56**
Mary's song, "The Magnificat," after she learned that she would be the mother of the Savior

**Luke 1:68-79**
Zechariah's song after the birth of his son, John the Baptist

**Luke 2:14**
The song of the angels at the birth of Jesus

**Acts 16:25**
Paul and Silas' song while in prison

**Romans 15:9**
Paul's quote of Psalm 18:49 to teach that the singing of psalms brings praise to God

**Ephesians 5:19; Colossians 3:16**
Paul's letter to the Ephesians tells the people to speak to each other with psalms, hymns, and spiritual songs

**James 5:13**
James commands those who are happy to sing

**Revelation 5:9-10**
The new song sung by the believers in heaven to glorify God

**Revelation 14:1-3**
The song of the 144,000

Allow the students to take turns selecting a slip of paper and drawing the story named on it on a chalkboard or a piece of newsprint. The rest of the participants will attempt to guess what is being drawn. After the story has been identified, read the Scripture verses to the group. If possible, find hymns based on these passages, and sing them after each illustration.

# Respond to a Recording

## Materials

► Bible(s)
► Equipment to play music
► Recordings of music

## Method

Music, available in many formats, is a wonderful teaching tool. Set the mood for a story, such as a lesson on the life of David, by playing a recording of harp music.

Review a theme by incorporating a symphonic poem technique. Listen to a musical selection, such as *Carnival of the Animals* by Saint Saëns and match its movements to the parts of a passage like the narrative of Noah. Play three to five different parts of the recording and ask the group to respond by naming or writing the section of the story that comes to mind when they hear the music.

Include music in a unit on feelings. Explore with the learners how they feel when they hear various types of music. Invite the participants to listen to different kinds of music. Play recordings that range from calypso to classical, rag to rock, and pop to polka. Ask if fast, peppy music helps them feel happy or if slow, solemn music makes them sad. Inquire about the type of music that makes them feel calm and peaceful. Encourage the children to share their feelings with the group. Assure them that it is all right for everyone to have different responses and reactions.

# Sing Old Testament Stories

## Materials

► Bible(s)
► Children's Songbooks
► Hymnals

## Method

Teach a lesson about an Old Testament character, such as David, by learning and singing songs about the person. Read the story in the Bible and then look through children's songbooks and church hymnals to find lyrics that tell the story through music. For example, songs such as "Little David Play On Your Harp" and "Only a Boy Named David" share information about David's life, while numerous versions of "Psalm 23" offer insight into David's work as a shepherd and inspiration about his worship of God.

Sing songs to tell stories about the lives of more Old Testament people. There are many songs written about Noah, Moses, Daniel, and others. *Joseph and the Amazing Technicolor Dreamcoat* is an entire musical following Joseph's story in the book of Genesis. Learn Old Testament stories through song!

# Survey Faith Stories

## Materials

► Bible(s)
► Books of hymn stories
► Construction paper
► Hangers
► Hole punches
► Hymnals
► Markers
► Pencils or pens
► Ribbon, string, or yarn
► Scissors

## Method

Take special note of the stories of some of the great hymns of the faith. Interesting information on hymn texts and hymn writers is contained in books such as:

*101 Hymn Stories.* (Osbeck, Kenneth W. Grand Rapids, MI: Kregel Publications, 1982.)

*Hymn Stories for Children: The Apostles' Creed.* (Wezeman, Phyllis Vos and Anna L. Liechty. Grand Rapids, MI: Kregel Publications, 1995.)

*Hymn Stories for Children: The Christmas Season* (Advent, Christmas, Epiphany). (Wezeman, Phyllis Vos and Anna L. Liechty. Grand Rapids, MI: Kregel Publications, 1997.)

*Hymn Stories for Children: Lent and Easter.* (Wezeman, Phyllis Vos and Anna L. Liechty. Pittsburgh, PA: Logos Systems Associates, 2002.)

*Hymn Stories for Children: The Lord's Prayer.* (Wezeman, Phyllis Vos and Anna L. Liechty. Grand Rapids, MI: Kregel Publications, 1996.)

*Hymn Stories for Children: Resources for Children's Worship.* (Wezeman, Phyllis Vos and Anna L. Liechty. Grand Rapids, MI: Kregel Publications, 1995.)

*Hymn Stories for Children: Special Days and Holidays.* (Wezeman, Phyllis Vos and Anna L. Liechty. Grand Rapids, MI: Kregel Publications, 1994.)

*Hymn Stories for Children: Spirituals.* (Wezeman, Phyllis Vos and Anna L. Liechty. Pittsburgh, PA: Logos Systems Associates, 2004.)

*Hymn Stories for Children: The Ten Commandments.* (Wezeman, Phyllis Vos and Anna L. Liechty. Grand Rapids, MI: Kregel Publications, 1996.)

Choose several familiar songs and supply background material about the life of the composer and the meaning of the words. Invite the participants to make mobiles to illustrate the songs. Pick one song for the entire group to depict or have each person select a song to use.

Distribute construction paper, scissors, and markers. Have each person cut out three shapes. Instruct them to write the name of the song on one, to record information about the composer on the second, and to draw a picture portraying its message on the third. Punch a hole in the top of each piece. Pass out three lengths of ribbon, string, or yarn and a hanger to each individual. Help the children run the cord through the holes and attach the pieces to their hangers. Display the mobiles. If time allows, sing several of the songs.

# Take a Field Trip

## Materials

► Bible(s)
► Information on musical performances

## Method

Arrange a field trip to a musical event—local, regional, or even national or international—and explore and experience a Bible story or theme in this unique way.  Possibilities for seeing and hearing Bible stories include outings to college or community theater productions of plays such as *Joseph and the Amazing Technicolor Dream Coat* or *Godspell*, or to local church performances of children's musicals like *Get On Board Children* or *It's Cool In the Furnace*.  Offer an opportunity for praise and worship by attending concerts of sacred music presented by choirs, instrumentalists, or vocalists.  As a highlight of the Christmas or Easter season, hear the Scripture passages in a fresh way by attending a rendition of Handel's *Messiah*.  Study a theme, such as forgiveness, by viewing a touring company show like *Les Misérables*.  Take advantage of special opportunities to tell the story by attending musical events.

# Write New Words

## Materials

► Bible(s)
► Music to selected song(s)
► Paper
► Pencils or pens

## Method

Take a familiar song, write a new verse to the tune, and use the music to tell a story.  For example, use the chorus "Row, Row, Row Your Boat" to teach the story of David.  Hum the melody or sing the song with the children.  Invite them to think of new words to convey a message related to the topic.  Show them a sample stanza such as:

Little David play your harp,
play your harp and sing.
Give praise to God your Maker,
let earth and heaven ring.

Pass out paper and pencils.  Continue writing verses as long as the students are interested in the activity.  Sing the new songs together.  Compiling songbooks and sharing the music with other people may extend the messages.

# Telling the Story through Photography

Snap a photo; screen a film; sequence a series of pictures. Design a shoot; draw on a transparency; develop a documentary. Telling stories through techniques involving photography and projection includes many methods. Using photography to tell stories can also have many purposes. Pictures, in numerous formats, can pique interest, present information, provide clarification, prompt discussion, and promote action. Ten suggestions for using photography as a storytelling tool are provided. Develop others to meet specific curriculum needs and classroom circumstances.

# Construct a Calendar

## Materials

- Bible(s)
- Calendar pages
- Calendars
- Construction paper
- Glue
- Magazine pictures
- Paper, 8 ½" x 11"
- Rings, clip-type
- Scissors

## Method

Calendars contain interesting and informative items. Besides recording months, weeks, and days, listing holidays, and providing information about special events, calendars often display beautiful photographs. Regardless of the subject, there seems to be a calendar with pictures to illustrate it. Make and use calendar pages as a way to review Bible stories connected with church year, holiday, and seasonal themes.

Complete the illustrations in one or two sessions or prepare one picture a month and compile the calendar for use during the next year. Regardless of the time frame for construction, select one Bible story or verse for each month. Write one passage on each of twelve 8 ½" x 11" pieces of white paper. Cut photographs from magazines, old calendars, and previous church school materials and attach them to the pages to illustrate each verse. Glue each sheet to the center of a 9" x 12" piece of construction paper. Attach a blank calendar page for each month up-side-down on the backside of each picture. In the same place on all sheets of paper, punch holes in the top and bottom of each piece of construction paper. Reinforce the holes. After the pages are assembled, put clip rings through the holes. Use the calendars for curriculum enrichment and for classroom activities.

# Develop a Design

## Materials

- ► Bible(s)
- ► Box top lids or cardboard
- ► Hydrogen peroxide
- ► Items related to lesson
- ► Measuring cup
- ► Plastic wrap
- ► Solar print paper
- ► Tape, cellophane
- ► Water

## Method

When telling the story of Creation or teaching a lesson on care of the earth, take pictures without using a camera. Purchase a package of solar print paper from a camera or a hobby shop. Open the package in a dark place and put a sheet on a piece of cardboard or set it inside of a box lid. Place an item related to the story, such as a flower or a leaf, on the paper. Tape it in place or cover it with clear plastic wrap. Set the paper in the sun for a few minutes (check the package directions for the exact time). Take the project inside, remove the items, and look at the design that was formed.

Make the pictures permanent by dipping them in a solution of one-fourth cup hydrogen peroxide and two cups water. Rinse the paper in cool water and blot it dry.

# Feature Film Festivals

## Materials

- ► Bible(s)
- ► Films on selected subject(s)
- ► Projector
- ► Screen

## Method

Hold a film festival. Pick a theme and show resources pertaining to it for one or several meetings. Movies spanning a wide range of topics are available from agencies, colleges, denominations, distributors, internet video sites, libraries, organizations, resource centers, school systems, and video stores. Use them to tell stories. Short audio-visuals are great to use when introducing a discussion, beginning a meeting, or illustrating a specific topic. Mid-length videos, running twenty to thirty minutes, include many sacred and secular themes. Feature films, an hour or longer, may need to be shown in special sessions.

There are many things to remember when showing a film. Of course, preview resources before showing them. Be sure that the equipment is in proper working order. In addition to a projector and a screen, assemble materials such as adapters, extension cords, flashlights, and extra bulbs. Also, be certain that someone who knows how to use the equipment and how to correct problems is with the operator. When the show starts, check that everyone can both see and hear the film.

# Manufacture a Movie

## Materials

▶ Bible(s)
▶ Equipment to produce film
▶ Equipment to project film
▶ Resource materials

## Method

Tell a biblical, historical, or modern day story by making a movie. Form a production company to plan and prepare resources on social justice topics affecting the congregation and the community. Learn more about issues such as drugs, homelessness, hunger, and pollution from books, field trips, and speakers. Then, put the results on film.

Before the session, obtain a camera to produce the film and equipment to project it. Be sure the equipment operates properly. Produce a video statement on the chosen topic. Incorporate creative methods for the presentation such as drama, games, and music. Allow time for the group to write the script and to hold a brief rehearsal. If there are a large number of participants, organize them into small groups and have each team create a scene. Record the segments. Show the finished product(s) to groups from the congregation and the community.

# Mount a Message

## Materials

► Computer, tablet, or smart phone

## Method

Social media, in many platforms, is a boon for sharing stories through photography. Use many of the following options, as well as others as they are created, to raise awareness on certain topics and to teach lessons on specific stories. Options include, but are not limited to:

### Email Programs
An email service, such as Constant Contact or MailChimp, is a low cost way to share stories in the form of news, pictures, and updates on various topics. Include information and photos in the body of the email rather than sending it as an attachment.

### Microblogging Sites
Twitter allows the user 140 characters—which can include pictures and videos—to share a brief message. Tumblr is an additional popular microblogging site.

### Photo Sharing Sites
Flikr, Instagram, and Pinterest are examples of sites for sharing pictures and for gathering collections of photos on various themes.

### Publishing Sites
Blogger and WordPress are examples of sites for blogs which can include photos to support the content of the posts.

### Social Networking Sites
Facebook is a good forum for sharing information, as well as photos and videos, of past, present, and future events.

### Video Sharing Sites
YouTube and Vimeo are examples of sites where video stories on countless themes can be posted for people to view.

### Websites
Develop and use a website as an interactive storytelling tool. Include opportunities for engagement and participation for and with those who visit the site.

In general, remember that social media is just one—of many—constantly changing ways to use photography as a storytelling tool.

# Picture with Polaroid

## Materials

- ▶ Albums
- ▶ Bible(s)
- ▶ Bulletin board
- ▶ Camera, digital or instant
- ▶ Film for instant-type camera
- ▶ Poster board
- ▶ Printer for digital camera
- ▶ Tacks or tape

## Method

After presenting the theme of a lesson, send the participants on a photo scavenger hunt. Although the activity can be done with digital photos, another approach would be to use instant cameras so there can be immediate results. If digital or other types of cameras are used, the pictures might need to be printed and shared at another session. Choose a Scripture passage, for example, the Beatitudes. Assign individuals or small groups to illustrate each one. Specify a time limit, ranging from thirty minutes to one week, to complete the project. When viewing each picture, discussion may center on why the student took the picture, how it relates to the topic, and what it means to him or her. The goal of the activity is not photographic excellence, but relevance. Display the pictures in albums, on poster board, or on bulletin boards. Examples of ways in which God's love is shown in the community, or documentation of a neighborhood renewal project, may be used with this photo method of storytelling.

# Project Some People

## Materials

- ▶ Acetate transparencies
- ▶ Bible(s)
- ▶ Overhead projector
- ▶ Permanent markers
- ▶ Resource materials
- ▶ Screen

## Method

Look up and discuss information on several of the people connected with the history of the church, such as Saint Augustine, Oscar Romero, and Pope John XXIII. Illustrate their stories by using permanent markers and drawing pictures on acetate transparencies. Assign each participant a particular person to depict. If freehand drawing is not an option for the group, make the transparencies by tracing pictures from books or by a copy machine process. Color and add details to the scenes. Take turns placing the transparencies on an overhead projector. As the drawings are displayed, invite the learners to re-tell, recite, or read stories about the people who contributed to their Christian heritage.

# Segue a Scene

## Materials

► Bible(s)
► Clothesline (optional)
► Clothespins (optional)
► Posters
► Teaching pictures

## Method

If teaching pictures from church school curricula and purchased sets have been accumulated through the years, use them to tell a story. Many parishes have organized these resources according to Bible stories and themes, making them easy to find for teaching purposes. To extend and reinforce understanding of a particular Bible story, challenge the learners to put a series of pictures in the proper sequence. Or clip a set of pictures to a clothesline. Ask different people to describe what is happening in each scene and tell the entire story in this way.

# Show Some Slides

## Materials

► Bible(s)
► Camera, digital, and/or graphs, illustrations, and pictures from various sources
► Computer
► PowerPoint or other presentation software
► Projector
► Screen

## Method

A series of slides with the right timing, music, and narration is a powerful communication tool. Put together a presentation, a series of slides, to tell or enhance a story. Utilize PowerPoint, Keynote, or other presentation software, which help to design graphs, pictures, and text that can be shared with an audience.

When studying stories about Jesus' ministry, project slides of Bible lands, available from people who have traveled there or from school supply sources. Recreate and photograph a Scripture story to share as slides. The Christmas story, Palm Sunday account, or narrative of David and Goliath lend themselves well to this type of activity. Divide the story into scenes, choose or create props and costumes, and assign and practice parts. Snap pictures of each scene. Set up a projector and screen and show the visualized story. Narration and music may be recorded or presented live.

In addition, try using presentation slides in learning centers as starters for projects or as step-by-step instructions for teaching activities.

# Snap a Shot

## Materials

- Bible(s)
- Construction paper
- Glue
- Hole punch (optional)
- Magnetic tape (optional)
- Pattern for crest
- Pencils
- Photographs
- Poster board
- Scissors
- String or yarn

## Method

Help the participants tell their own story by making crest collages from photographs they have accumulated over the years. In advance, ask each person to bring a variety of pictures that will help share his or her life story. Snapshots should span the time from birth through the present, and include pictures of favorite memories, family, friends, hobbies, and special events.

Tell the group that crests are emblems, used primarily during the Middle Ages, to designate specific families or people, and to impart information about their lives. They are often attached to clothing, dishes, doors, flags, and homes. Begin the project by cutting a crest shape from poster board for each participant. Direct the group members to cover the paper by cutting and gluing pictures to it that illustrate their life stories. Words and symbols, such as a cross, may be made from construction paper and added to the pieces. Attach a magnetic strip to the backside or tie a string or yarn from the top of the crest for hanging. Display the crests in the classroom and invite each person to share his or her story with the entire group. If this activity is used with older youth suggest that they create a spiritual autobiography on their crests.

# Telling the Story
## through
# Puppetry

Puppetry is the art of bringing an inanimate object to "life" and communicating a message with it. This ancient medium has been used around the world to educate, to enlighten, and to entertain. In Southeast Asia, shadow puppets are tools that dramatize religious epics. In Europe, priests introduced the marionette to help people visualize Bible stories. In Africa, carved figures are devices that help to transmit oral history.

Puppets are used in congregations in worship, education, outreach, and nurture ministries.

They make announcements, play roles during children's sermons, illustrate songs, teach Sunday School lessons, highlight seasonal programs, visit nursing homes, and much more.

Ideas for ten projects, which illustrate the story of Moses, focus on puppets that can be quickly and easily constructed from low-cost or no-cost readily available items. Six basic puppet styles—body, finger, hand, marionette, rod, and shadow are represented in the examples.

# Pop-up a Puppet

## Materials

- Bible(s)
- Construction paper
- Glue
- Markers
- Paper cups
- Pencils
- Scissors

## Method

Moses, an Israelite baby, was placed in a basket and hidden in the reeds to protect him from being killed by Egypt's Pharaoh. Found by Pharaoh's daughter, Moses was taken to the palace and raised as her son.

Illustrate this story with a pop-up rod puppet baby and basket. Gather a paper cup, pencil, scissors, glue, construction paper, and markers. Decorate a cup to resemble the basket. Push a pencil up through the bottom of the cup. Using construction paper, draw and cut out the shape of a baby. Glue it to the top of the pencil. Move the pencil up and down to hide or display the baby.

# Speak with a Shepherd

## Materials

- Bible(s)
- Construction paper
- Craft sticks or paint stirrers
- Fiberfil®
- Foam peanuts
- Glue
- Markers
- Paper plates
- Scissors
- Tape

## Method

When Moses got older he worked as a shepherd. Talk about this part of Moses' life by making paper plate rod puppet sheep.

Using markers or construction paper, create a sheep's face on the backside of a paper plate. Add a three dimensional material, such as curled paper, foam peanuts, or fluffy stuffing, around the facial features to make the wool. Attach a craft stick or paint stirrer to the front of the paper plate and use the rod to operate the puppet.

# Build a Bush

## Materials

- ► Bible(s)
- ► Cellophane, various colors
- ► Hole punches
- ► Poster board
- ► Scissors
- ► Shadow puppet screen
- ► Straws
- ► Tape

## Method

One day God spoke to Moses from a burning bush and said that Moses would free the Israelites from slavery and lead them to a new land. Create the burning bush as a shadow puppet and tell the story.

Cut a bush shape out of poster board. Tape red, yellow, and orange cellophane behind the cutout areas. Form a rod by taping the top inch, or bendable portion, of a straw to the center of the back of the puppet. Share stories behind a shadow screen such as white paper inside the opening of a box or white muslin or cotton over a frame.

# Accent on Aaron

## Materials

- ► Bible(s)
- ► Construction paper
- ► Milk cartons, half-gallon size
- ► Scissors
- ► String
- ► Tape

## Method

Since Moses was afraid, God told him to take his brother Aaron as his spokesperson. Create a movable mouth puppet of Aaron from a half-gallon milk carton.

Clean the carton and tape the spout shut. Cover the carton with construction paper, the top third with a facial colored paper, and the remaining portion with a color to suggest clothing. Add decorations. Cut through the carton on the front and two sides along the mouth line. With masking tape, secure a string near the top on the back, or uncut side. Pull and release the string and the puppet will appear to talk.

# Ponder with Pharaoh

## Materials

- Bottles
- Duct tape
- Fabric scraps
- Fake fur
- Felt
- Fiberfil®
- Glue
- Paper towel tubes
- Scissors
- Yarn

## Method

When Moses told Pharaoh to let God's people go, Egypt's ruler commanded the Israelite slaves to work even harder. Tell this story using a bottle puppet figure representing Pharaoh.

Clean and de-label a bottle. Place a paper towel tube on the pouring spout of the bottle and tape the two pieces together. Using felt scraps, cut eyes and a mouth and glue them in place. Use the handle as the nose. Make hair from yarn, fake fur, or Fiberfil® and glue it to the top of the puppet's head. Choose a large square of fabric, cut a small hole in the center, and slide the paper towel tube through it. Tape the fabric to the neck. Add trims. Hold the puppet by the rod and use it to tell Pharaoh's story.

# Plague with Problems

## Materials

- Bible(s)
- Construction paper or poster board
- Glue
- Markers
- Scissors

## Method

God sent plagues on the Egyptians to try to convince Pharaoh to let the Israelites go. Devise a way to remember the first nine plagues through the use of finger puppets.

Draw a picture of each plague on a piece of construction paper or poster board. Cut them out. Cut a short strip of construction paper and form it into a loop that will fit snugly around the finger. Glue the ends of the paper together. Make one loop for each puppet. Glue the loops to the backs of the pictures. Place a puppet on each finger and use them to tell the story of the plagues.

# Exit the Egyptians

## Materials

- ► Bible(s)
- ► Fabric pieces
- ► Felt scraps
- ► Glue
- ► Plastic or wooden spoons
- ► Scissors

## Method

God had one more punishment for the Egyptians—their firstborn would be killed. Finally, Pharaoh demanded that Moses and the Israelites leave Egypt. God parted the Red Sea so the Israelites could cross safely, but when the Egyptians tried to walk through, the waters closed, and the Egyptians drowned. Tell the story by using spoon puppets.

Use a permanent marker to draw a face on the curved, bottom side of a plastic or wooden spoon. Make hair from yarn, cotton or felt and glue it to the top of the head. Glue a piece of fabric to the front of the spoon at the neck. Arms, made from pipe cleaners, can be twisted around the spoon.

# Include the Israelites

## Materials

- ► Bible(s)
- ► Cotton, fake fur, or yarn
- ► Fabric
- ► Felt
- ► Glue
- ► Scissors
- ► Socks
- ► Styrofoam balls, 3"

## Method

God provided for the Israelites as they journeyed to the "Promised Land." Make and use sock puppets to tell different segments of Scripture.

Form the head of the puppet from a three-inch Styrofoam ball. Cut a hole in the bottom of the ball, just large enough for the index finger to fit into it. Put the ball into the toe of a sock, with the hole at the bottom. Form facial features from felt and glue them to the sock. Add material for hair and costume. Operate the puppet by placing one hand inside the sock with the index finger in the hole.

# Send the Scouts

## Materials

► Bible(s)
► Cotton, fake fur, or yarn
► Fabric
► Felt
► Glue
► Paper tubes
► Scissors

## Method

When the Israelites finally arrived at the place God promised them, they were afraid to enter it. Only two—Joshua and Caleb—trusted God and told the people to go into the land. Make tube puppets to tell this story.

Select a paper tube for the project. Form the puppet face by cutting a piece of felt and gluing it to the top one-third of the tube. Cut facial features from felt scraps and glue them in place. Add cotton, fake fur, or yarn as hair and attach it to the top of the tube. Glue felt around the remainder of the tube to serve as the garment. Make arms from strips of cloth or felt and glue them to the sides of the tube. Apply a craft stick to the inside back of the tube to serve as the rod by which the puppet is operated.

# Meditate with Moses

## Materials

► Bible(s)
► Construction paper
► Cotton, fake fur, or yarn
► Fabric
► Glue
► Markers
► Newspaper
► Paper lunch bags
► Paper tubes
► Rubber bands
► Tape
► Scissors

## Method

At the end of his life, Moses sang a song of praise and thanks to God. Moses blessed the people and prayed that God would watch over them.

Make a stuffed paper bag rod puppet to use as Moses. Open a paper lunch bag. Crumple several sheets of newspaper, one at a time, and stuff them into the bag. Insert a paper tube into the center of the bag. Bunch the bag around the tube and secure it with a rubber band or tape. Draw facial features on one side of the bag or cut them from construction paper and glue them in place. Attach a variety of materials for hair and clothing. Hold the puppet by the tube, or rod, to share Moses' parting words.

# Telling the Story through Storytelling

"Storytelling is an art and, like all arts, it requires training and experience. However, anyone who is willing to take the time to find the right story and learn it well, and who has a sincere desire to share enjoyment of the story, can be a successful storyteller. A good part of our daily conversation is composed of stories, incidents, and anecdotes, for we are all storytellers a few steps removed from professional storytellers. Our language is somewhat less formalized, but we still share our experiences and emotions." (Augusta Baker and Ellin Greene. *Storytelling: Art and Technique.* New York: Bowker, 1977.)

Spotlight the art of oral storytelling to help people hear God's Word in a "new" way. Try any or all of the ten techniques for "Telling the Story through Storytelling."

# Communicate with Color

## Materials

- ► Bible(s)
- ► Construction paper, various colors
- ► Fabric, various colors

## Method

Think about the colors associated with a story and use them to help convey the message. Display or distribute pieces of colored fabric or paper at the appropriate places in the story.

In telling the narrative of Moses, for example, show a variety of colors to highlight various portions of the Scripture passage. Brown could illustrate the woven basket Moses' mother made, blue the water on which it floated, and green the bulrushes in which he was hidden. Purple might symbolize the royal palace in which Moses lived after Pharaoh's daughter found him, and red could stand for the bricks made during the difficult years in Egypt. Encourage the participants to experiment with using color to help tell a Bible story.

# Obtain an Object

## Materials

- ► Bible(s)
- ► Bags, baskets, or boxes
- ► Object(s) related to story

## Method

Use an object to introduce a story or several objects to illustrate various parts of a narrative. For example, display a crown of thorns at the beginning of a story about the crucifixion or show a stone at the start of the story of the empty tomb.

Another method would be to include bags, boxes, or baskets in the activity. For the account of the Ascension, place a picture of Jesus in one container, a cotton "cloud" in another, and a crown in the third. Distribute the bags to three different participants. Ask each person, one at a time, to remove the object inside. Invite the learners to guess the story to be shared. Another method would be to place all of the objects in one box. Remove each of them at the appropriate point in the story to serve as visual aids.

# Peruse the Paint

## Materials

- Bible(s)
- Bible story books
- Resources related to the topic

## Method

Provide a variety of books for the participants to explore. Suggest a story and have them locate it in Bible story books, various translations of the Bible, and religious magazines. Make children's books, comics, Braille materials, foreign language versions, and publications appropriate to the theme available for the group to examine. Be sure to select resources for children with a wide range of reading skills and to pick books with illustrations from which they can gather accurate information.

Encourage the children to prepare their own versions of the story from these sources and to tell it to the rest of the group.

# Pick a Partner

## Materials

- Bible(s)
- Names of older adults

## Method

Originate a project in which children share faith stories with older people in the congregation. In advance, obtain the names of several persons and set up a meeting time and place. Tell the students that they will have the privilege of visiting and sharing with these long-lived folks. Suggest conversation starters and questions to use during the session. For example, the youth may inquire about church school classes, worship services, and seasonal observances that took place when the seniors were in elementary school. Encourage discussion of the elderly person's fondest childhood memories associated with the story. Invite each child to tell portions of their partner's faith story to the entire group.

# React with Rhythm

## Materials

▶ Bible(s)
▶ Paper
▶ Pencils or pens

## Method

Enjoy God's Word by using rhythm and rhyme to tell a Scripture story. A rhythm or echo story is a participatory method in which the leader chants a line and the group repeats or echoes it back.

Choose a Bible story and write a rhythm story for it. Often these stories have eight beats to a line; however, sometimes more than one syllable is said to a beat. Several verses can be composed. Start the story by establishing a clapping rhythm to accompany the lines. A slap on the knees and a clap of the hands works well. Invite the group to repeat the rhythm. Chant the first line of the story to this rhythm and have the group echo it back. Continue telling the story in this manner.

An example of a rhythm story based on 1 Kings 17:1-7, the account of God's provisions for Elijah, is:

### Elijah: Protection and Provisions

Elijah of Tishbee in Galilee
brought God's message to Ahab,
   the King.
"There will be no dew or rainfall,
because you've done a terrible thing."

After Elijah brought the King the warning
God told the prophet to go and hide.
Elijah went to the brook called Cherith
with God, the Protector, at his side.

Then the brook became his water;
Meat and bread came every day.
It was brought to him by ravens.
God took care of him in every way.

# Read a Rebus

## *Materials*

► Bible(s)
► Markers
► Poster board

## *Method*

In a rebus story, illustrations are substituted for easily pictured words. This is an effective method to help children, especially young ones, remember a story. Select a short Bible passage containing terms that are easily depicted. Write it on a large piece of poster board if it is to be shared with an entire group or on individual sheets of paper that will be duplicated and distributed to each person in a class. Leave blank spaces where pictures will substitute for words. Draw a picture for each missing word or invite the children to participate in this process. For example, in the Easter story, draw an angel each time this word is mentioned or a tomb whenever there is a reference to this symbol. Read the story in unison, or have one person read the words and invite the rest of the listeners to respond by naming each picture as it appears.

# Review with Round Robin

## Materials

▶ Bible(s)

## Method

Round robin is a cooperative method of telling a story. In this approach, each participant adds a sentence or statement, or a certain number of words. As a way to introduce or review a lesson, invite the learners to make up a round robin story. If there are a large number of participants, have them add three to five words per person. If only a few people are involved, increase the number of words for each person to add. Continue until the story seems to be concluded or until the pupils run out of ideas. Following the story, supply any details that may have been skipped, and discuss some of the thoughts that were presented.

A round robin using the Old Testament story of Esther as the example might be:

Esther was a
beautiful young woman
who was chosen
to be queen.

When wicked Haman
plotted to destroy
the Jewish people,
Esther's cousin Mordecai
begged her to
ask the king
to save them.

Esther told him
that she was
a Jewish woman.

The Jewish people's
lives were saved
because of Queen
Esther's brave act.

# Study a Story

► Bible(s)
► Book(s) of stories

*Method*

In addition to preparing a story for a class or a group, each of us tells stories—usually many stories—everyday. Often we are unconscious of the fact that we are indeed storytellers. Try these basic steps in learning to tell stories to share during education, as well as worship events. With determination, practice, and experience, any leader can become an accomplished storyteller.

1. Select a good story. Pick one that will be enjoyable to learn. Be sure it is appropriate for the age level of the audience.

2. Read and re-read the story. Enjoy it, concentrate on it, and analyze it.

3. Read the story aloud.

4. Become familiar with the various parts of the story: the beginning, the middle, and the end. In the beginning the characters and the conflict are introduced. During the middle, or the body of the story, the conflict builds to a climax. In the end, the conclusion is presented.

5. Learn words and phrases that are essential to the story.

6. Imagine the sights and sounds of the story.

7. Add emphasis and pacing to enhance the words.

8. Practice aloud!

# Tape Record Tales

*Materials*

► Bible(s)
► Device for recording and playing a story

*Method*

Invite each participant to select the same or a different story and to make a recording of it to share with others. Assist the children as they practice and prepare what they will say.

Provide equipment for recording and playing a story, such as a smart phone or tablet. Guide each person as he or she speaks the story.

Share the recordings with shut-ins, absent classmates, or younger children or place the recordings in learning centers that correspond with various lessons and themes.

# Test More Techniques

## Materials

► Bible(s)

## Method

Try a new technique for telling tales. Learn a string story, add a magic trick, or illustrate the words by using origami or a cut-and-fold procedure. Enhance the story by delivering it in a unique way.

# Methods

## Art

Batik [Banners/Textiles]: Banner

Chalk [Art]: Illustrations

Diorama [Art]: Make

Flannelgraph [Art]: Make

Flip Chart [Art]: Make

Illustrations/Pictures [Art]: Display

Mobile [Art]: Make

Mobile [Music]: Make to illustrate hymn stories

Mural [Art]: Sequence Story

Puzzle Pieces [Music]: Fit together to illustrate Christmas carols

Puzzles [Art]: Make

Rebus Story [Storytelling]: Write

Rhythm Instruments [Music]: Construct

Story Dial [Art]: Illustrate/Tell Story

Video Box [Art]: Make

## Banners/Textiles

Bags [Banners/Textiles]: Combine as banner

Batik [Banners/Textiles]: Make banners

Branch [Banners/Textiles]: Banner background

Computer [Banners/Textiles]: Make banners

Fabric [Banners/Textiles]: Make banners

Fabric pieces [Banners/Textiles]: Decorate individual pieces; combine as banner

Paper [Banners/Textiles]: Make banners

Ribbon [Banners/Textiles]: Combine individual pieces as banner

Shade [Banners/Textiles]: Decorate as banner

Stitching [Banners/Textiles]: Stitch design on banner

Windsock [Banners/Textiles]: Batik banner

# Creative Writing

ABC [Creative Writing]: Write

Alliteration [Creative Writing]: Write

Cinquain [Creative Writing]: Write

Couplet [Creative Writing]: Write

Dada [Creative Writing]: Write

Diamond [Creative Writing]: Write

Haiku [Creative Writing]: Write

Lantern [Creative Writing]: Write

Quatrain [Creative Writing]: Write

Rhythm Story [Storytelling]: Write

Tanka [Creative Writing]: Write

Words to familiar tunes [Music]: Write

# Dance/Gesture/ Movement

Body Sculpture [Dance/Gesture/Movement]: Positions

Circle Dance [Dance/Gesture/Movement]: Exclude/Include People

Creative Movement/Improvisation [Dance/ Gesture/Movement]: Interpret poem/ prayer/song/speech/story

Dance-a-Thon [Dance/Gesture/Movement]: Raise money for a cause

Folk Dance [Dance/Gesture/Movement]: Great Commission; Learn

Game (Follow the Leader) [Dance/Gesture/ Movement]: Lead/Play

Gesture [Dance/Gesture/Movement]: Interpretation

Popular Dance (Macarena) [Dance/Gesture/ Movement]: Movements/Words to match story

Ritual [Dance/Gesture/Movement]: Movement; Passing the Peace

Sign Language [Dance/Gesture/Movement]: Sign/Story

# Drama

Action Story [Drama]: Gesture/Movement/ Words

Characterization of Bible Passage [Drama]: Write Scripture script

Choral Reading [Drama]: Prepare or present

Costumes/Props [Drama]: Perform

Event [Drama]: Attend performance or watch video

Improvisation [Drama]: Improvise a story

Original Script [Drama]: Write

Role Play [Drama]: Situations

Scripts [Drama]: Try techniques

TV News Show Format [Drama]: Interview

# Games

Bingo [Games]: Make/Play

Board Game [Games]: Make/Play

Concentration [Games]: Make/Play

Cooperative Games [Games]: Learn/Play

Fact/Fiction Cards (Questions) [Games]: Make/Play

Follow the Leader [Dance/Gesture/ Movement]: Sheep/Shepherd

Ice Breakers [Games]: Introductions/Play

Jeopardy (Questions) [Games]: Make/Play

Links (Construction Paper Chain) [Games]: Make/Play/Vocabulary Words

Lotto (Concentration) [Games]: Make/Play

Musical Chairs (Cooperative Games) [Games]: Play

Paper/Pencil Games [Games]: Alphabet Challenge ▪ Category Columns ▪ Code ▪ Connect the Dots ▪ Crossword Puzzle ▪ Matching ▪ Scrambled Words ▪ Tic Tac Toe ▪ Who Am I? ▪ Word Find ▪ Word Pictures ▪ Word Search

Questions (Fact/Fiction; Jeopardy) [Games]: Make/Play

Relay [Games]: Items related to story

Scavenger Hunt [Games]: Items related to story

Win, Lose, or Draw [Music]: New Testament stories/Music

## Music

Christmas Carols [Music]: Puzzle pieces

Concert [Music]: Organize

Field Trips [Music]: Attend performances

Hymn Stories [Music]: Mobiles

New Testament Music [Music]: Win, Lose, or Draw Game

Old Testament Stories [Music]: Find songs

Psalms [Music]: Chant antiphonally

Recordings [Music]: Respond

Rhythm Instruments [Music]: Construct

Words to familiar tunes [Music]: Write

## Photography

Calendar [Photography]: Make

Films [Photography]: Show

Movies [Photography]: Make

Overhead Transparencies [Photography]: Make

Photographs [Photography]: Take

Polaroid Pictures [Photography]: Take

PowerPoint/Slide Show [Photography]: Produce

Social Media Platforms [Photography]: Create

Solar Prints [Photography]: Make

Teaching Pictures [Photography]: Display

# Puppetry

Bottle Rod Puppet [Puppetry]: Make

Finger Puppet [Puppetry]: Make

Milk Carton Moveable Mouth Hand Puppet [Puppetry]: Make

Paper Bag/Tube Puppet [Puppetry]: Make

Paper Plate Rod Puppet [Puppetry]: Make

Pop-Up Rod Puppet [Puppetry]: Make

Shadow Puppet [Puppetry]: Make

Sock/Styrofoam Ball Hand Puppet [Puppetry]: Make

Spoon Rod Puppet [Puppetry]: Make

Tube Rod Puppet [Puppetry]: Make

# Storytelling

Books [Storytelling]: Read and tell

Color Story [Storytelling]: Tell

Interviews [Storytelling]: Children and older adults

Objects [Storytelling]: Object lessons

Rebus Story [Storytelling]: Write

Round Robin [Storytelling]: Create

Rhythm Story [Storytelling]: Write

Story Dial [Art]: Illustrate/Tell Story

Storytelling Steps [Storytelling]: Learn

Tape Recorded Stories [Storytelling]: Tape

Various Methods [Storytelling]: Origami

100 CREATIVE TECHNIQUES FOR TEACHING BIBLE STORIES

# Resources

*Note: Some are classic resources for the method*

## Art

Erickson, Donna. *Prime Time Together ... with Kids – Creative Ideas, Activities, Games, and Projects.* Minneapolis, MN: Augsburg, 1989.

Mackenzie, Joy. *The Big Book of Bible Crafts and Projects.* Nashville, TN: Impact Books, 1981.

Stroh, Deborah. *Christ's Kids Create! 102 Favorite Crafts for Kids 4 to 14.* St. Louis, MO: Concordia Publishing House, 1992.

## Banners/Textiles

Blair, Margot Carter and Cathleen Ryan. *Banners and Flags – How to Sew a Celebration.* New York: Harcourt Brace Jovanovich, 1977.

Editors. *Symbol Patterns – Ideas for banners, posters, bulletin boards.* Minneapolis, MN: Augsburg Publishing House, 1981.

Ortegel, Adelaide, SP. *Banners and Such.* Saratoga, CA: Resource Publications, 1980.

## Creative Writing

Keithahn, Mary Nelson. *Creative Ideas for Teaching: Learning through Writing.* Prescott, AZ: Educational Ministries, Inc., 1987.

Sutherland, Zena and May Hill Arbuthnot. "Poetry." *Children and Books, 7th Edition.* Glenview, IL: Scott, Foresman, 1986.

## Dance/Gesture/ Movement

Daniels, Marilyn. *The Dance in Christianity.* New York: Paulist Press, 1981.

De Sola, Carla. *The Spirit Moves – Handbook of Dance and Prayer.* Austin, TX: The Sharing Company, 1977.

Ortegel, Sister Adelaide. *A Dancing People.* West Lafayette, IN: The Center for Contemporary Celebration, 1976.

## Drama

Glavich, Sr. Mary Kathleen, SND. *Gospel Plays for Students – 36 Scripts for Education and Worship.* Mystic, CT: Twenty-Third Publications, 1989.

Litherland, Janet. *Getting Started in Drama Ministry – A Complete Guide to Christian Drama.* Colorado Springs, CO: Meriwether Publishing Ltd., 1988.

Robertson, Everett. *Introduction to Church Drama.* Nashville, TN: Convention Press, 1978.

## Games

Fluegelman, Andrew, Editor. *The New Games Book: Play Hard, Play Fair, Nobody Hurt.* San Francisco, CA: The Headlands Press, 1976.

Grunfeld, Frederic V. *Games of the World: How to Make Them, How to Play Them, How They Came to Be.* Zurich, Switzerland: Swiss Committee for UNICEF, 1982.

Orlick, Tom. *The Cooperative Sports and Games Book.* New York: Pantheon Books, 1978.

## Music

Diagram Group for UNICEF. *Musical Instruments of the World.* New York: Facts on File Publications, 1976.

McLean, Margaret. *Make Your Own Musical Instruments.* Minneapolis, MN: Lerner Publications, 1988.

Wezeman, Phyllis Vos and Anna L. Liechty. *Hymn Stories for Children: Special Days and Holidays.* Grand Rapids, MI: Kregel Publications, 1994.

## Photography

Le Baron, John and Phillip Miller. *Portable Video: A Production Guide for Young People.* Englewood Cliffs, NJ: Prentice-Hall, 1982.

Wezeman, Phyllis Vos. *The Christmas Scene Revisited.* Brea, CA: Educational Ministries, Inc., 1991.

## Puppetry

Engler, Larry and Carol Fijan. *Making Puppets Come Alive.* New York: Taplinger, 1973.

Renfro, Nancy. *Puppet Shows Made Easy.* Austin, TX: Nancy Renfro Studios, 1984.

Wezeman, Phyllis Vos. *Puppet Projects for Scripture Stories.* Prescott, AZ: Educational Ministries, Inc., 1995.

## Storytelling

Bauer, Caroline Feller. *Handbook for Storytellers.* Chicago: American Library Association, 1977.

Sawyer, Ruth. *The Way of the Storyteller.* New York: Dover, 1951.

Shedlock, Marie L. *The Art of the Storyteller.* New York: Dover, 1951.

100 CREATIVE TECHNIQUES FOR TEACHING BIBLE STORIES

# About the Author

As a religious educator, Phyllis Wezeman has served as Director of Christian Nurture at a downtown congregation in South Bend, Indiana, Executive Director of the Parish Resource Center of Michiana, and Program Coordinator for ecumenical and interfaith organizations in Indiana and Michigan.

In academics, Phyllis has been Adjunct Faculty in the Education Department at Indiana University South Bend and in the Department of Theology at the University of Notre Dame. She is an Honorary Professor of the Saint Petersburg (Russia) State University of Pedagogical Art where she taught methods courses. She has also been guest lecturer at the Shanghai Teachers College in China.

As founder of the not-for-profit Malawi Matters, Inc., she develops and directs HIV & AIDS Education programs with thousands of volunteers in nearly 200 villages in Malawi, Africa including "Creative Methods of HIV & AIDS Education," "Culture & HIV-AIDS," and "Equipping Women/ Empowering Girls."

Author or co-author of over 1,950 articles and books, she has written for over 80 publishers.

Phyllis served as President of Active Learning Associates, Inc. and as a consultant or board member to numerous organizations such as the American Bible Society, Church World Service, and the Peace Child Foundation; leader of a youth exchange program to Russia and the Ukraine; and Project Director for four Lilly Worship Renewal grants. She is the recipient of three Distinguished Alumni Awards and recipient of the Aggiornamento Award from the Catholic Library Association.

Wezeman holds undergraduate degrees in Business, Communications, and General Studies and an MS in Education from Indiana University South Bend.

Phyllis and her husband Ken (who met when they were in second and third grade in elementary school) have three children, five grandchildren, and a great-grandson.

## 52 Interactive Bible Stories

### *A Collection of Action, Echo, Rhythm, and Syllable Stories*

Participants will love these playful ways of expressing Scripture through a variety of storytelling techniques:. This delightful collection tells Bible stories in creative, interactive ways that will engage anyone from the toddlers through adulthood. They are a great way to add life to classes or retreat-like experiences. These playful stories involve the learner in the process and ensure that the Bible story is understood an internalized.

74 PAGES • 8½"x11" • PW100

## Experience the Saints

*Activities for Multiple Intelligences*

Eight activities per saint, each based on a different learning intelligence. Includes whole family and general classroom guides, with reproducible handouts.

- Vol. 1: Patrick, James, Hildegard of Bingen • PW201
- Vol. 2: Francis, Clare, Margaret of Scotland • PW202
- Vol. 3: Joan of Arc, Thomas Becket, Agnes • PW203
- Vol. 4: Peter, Catherine of Siena, Scholastica • PW204

200 PAGES PER VOLUME • 8½"x11"

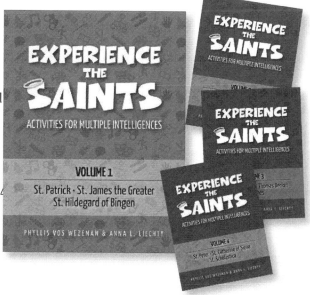

## Praying by Number

*Creative Prayer Lessons & Activities*

- Two volumes, with 20 activities each.
- Fun and faith-filled ways to teach children and families how to talk to God.

76 PAGES PER VOLUME • 8½"x11" • PW110 / PW111

# Seasons by Step: A Week-by-Week Thematic Approach

*Use these creative approaches to explore a theme in-depth over the course of a season through Scripture.* Each includes **talking points for children's messages, at-home family activities, artwork** for weekly symbols, and more.

## Know Chocolate for Lent *(Lent & Holy Week)*

Uses the growing and manufacturing process of chocolate as a metaphor for the growth of faith and discipleship in the Christian life. Adult formation materials for a parish-wide approach are sold separately. • 80 PAGES • LR119

## God's Family Tree *(Lent & Holy Week)*
### Tracing the Story of Salvation

Tells the story of God's people as they struggle to find faith and hope for life through the symbols of trees found in Scripture. Includes optional Easter pageant and classroom activities. • 114 PAGES • LR116

## In the Name of the Master *(Advent/Christmas/Epiphany)*
### Sharing the Story of Christ

Uses a variation of the Advent wreath that uses fruits as symbols for the many names of God's Masterpiece, Jesus. Help your kids & families go deeper as they light their Advent candles each week. • 37 PAGES • LR108

• • • • • • • • • • • • • • • • • • • • • • • • • • • • • • • • • • • • • • • • • • •

## Joy to the World
### International Christmas Crafts & Customs

Dozens of activities, from 12 countries that you can use again and again. Develop an appreciation for the contributions of the peoples of all lands and races to the celebration of Christmas. • 159 PAGES • 8½"x11" • LR104

## Ideas A-Z
### Crafts & Activities for Advent, Christmas, & Epiphany

Offers different theme or learning approach for each letter of the alphabet. Great ideas for intergenerational activities, lesson plans, or worship experiences. • 94 PAGES • 8½"x11" • PW102

## Finding Your Way after Your Child Dies

Offers parents a comforting way to grieve. Easily adapted for use in small and large group settings such as a support group, prayer service, or family ministry session. • 192 PAGES • IC937005

## http://pastoral.center/phyllis-vos-wezeman

 **The Pastoral Center** *Pastoral ministers serving pastoral ministers*

http://pastoral.center • resources@pastoralcenter.com • Call us at 844-727-8672 (M-F 9am-5pm CT)

Made in the USA
Columbia, SC
21 November 2018